THE
THREE ART

CW00473927

ACKNOWLEDGMENTS

I wish to thank the National Library of Wales for making available to me the original works of William Stukeley and John Gordon, with the several drawings of Arthur's O'n.

I thank Dr. Toby Griffin for permitting me to use some brief quotations from his book *Names from the Dawn of British Legend.*

I thank Christina Negus for the photographs of green men and permission to quote an extract from her text entitled *The Knights Templar and the Green Man'* in 3rd Stone.

I thank Mr Wade Miller-Knight for permission to refer to his interpretation of the title and first verse of the poem Preiddeu Annwn.

I also wish to acknowledge that the writing of this book has been facilitated by two works: firstly *the Celtic Sources of the Arthurian Quest* by Coe and Young which contains a comprehensive collection of Welsh, Gaelic and Latin texts with facing translations; secondly Bartrum's *Welsh Classical Dictionary* which brings together much of the available data about people and places in early Welsh history and tradition. Having located the various texts from these works, I have gone back to the original sources in almost all cases. *Taliesin Poems, The Black Book of Carmarthen,* and *Peredur,* with translations by Meirion Pennar have also been useful sources.

THE THREE ARTHURS:
HISTORY, LEGEND AND QUEST

by

Derek Bryce

ISBN 1 86143 143 0

Published in Aberystwyth in 2006
by the author
and distributed by

LLANERCH PRESS,
Penbryn Lodge, Cribyn, Lampeter.
Web www.llanerch-publishers.co.uk
E-Mail enquiries@llanerch-publishers.co.uk

CONTENTS

Preface and Introduction

There have been umpteen books published on Arthur during the past fifty years. I can think of no apology for writing this one, so here it is. I have tried to cover slightly different ground by considering Arthur in three rôles; first as the assumed and generally accepted Arthur of history; second as the Arthur of medieval legend depicted as a famous king with a following of knights in shining armour; and thirdly Arthur as guru or spiritual head of an order of chivalry.

The Arthur of history is known to us from a few entries in the ancient books of Wales and from early histories such as the *Historia Brittonum* or *History of Britain* attributed to Nennius, the oldest known text of which probably dates back to the early ninth century. There are also some medieval histories that include references to the historical Arthur, based on known sources such as Nennius, lost sources, or more doubtful ones. From a later date we have the Welsh Triads which include references to the early period, and other mediaeval Welsh literature and poetry which sometimes has historical or geographical references hidden here and there. The idea of a historical Arthur as well as a legendary character has been held by many from William of Malmesbury, writing in the twelfth century, until modern times, but there are others who doubt or refuse to believe that the historical Arthur ever existed, and I shall take up this matter in a later chapter.

The Arthur of medieval romance is first known to us from Geoffrey of Monmouth's famous *History of the Kings of Britain* which contains imaginative fiction, embellishment and mis-translated history, and which spawned a plethora of new tales of quest and adventure, of which the best-known are Mallory's *Morte d'Arthur* and Tennyson's *Idylls of the King*. In Wales there are also the mediaeval romances such as the *Four Branches of the Mabinogi* and some other tales that are loosely but incorrectly termed 'Mabinogion.' Some of these tales include Arthur.

Hints at the spiritual rôle of Arthur as guru can be seen in a poem in the Book of Taliesin commonly known as the *Spoils of Annwn*, in the Welsh tale of *Peredur* which predates the work of Geoffrey, and in the famous *Quest of the Holy Grail*.

Questions that arise from the foregoing include; firstly, to what extent is there evidence for Arthur as a dark-age war leader; secondly, to what extent were the medieval fictions based on the historical character, events and geography, and thirdly, what was the significance of the emergence and development of the literature of the knightly ideal and of the famous *Quest of the Grail* and did any of this come from earlier sources, or was it purely medieval fiction, albeit truth-bearing in its symbolism.

I shall try to present reasoned arguments aimed at clarifying some of these points. I apologise for a certain amount of repetition in this book, but I think it better to repeat some items than to keep referring the reader back to them in earlier chapters. Readers are reminded that there is a vast literature on this subject and that the last word will probably never be written, and like many others who have written on this topic, I cannot claim to be right about everything I have written. I hope nevertheless that this little work will lead some readers to a clearer understanding of some aspects of 'Arthuriana.'

Derek Bryce, 2005.

1. THE ARTHUR OF HISTORY

The probable Arthur of history is quite different from the one of mediaeval romance. He and his times are known to us from just a few sources; firstly from a few mentions in ancient Welsh poetry and in later poems such as the *Welsh Triads;* secondly in the dark-age histories of Gildas who was his contemporary but never mentioned him by name, and of Nennius in which a catalogue of Arthur's battles is given; thirdly in mediaeval hagiography, although not all references to Arthur in the Lives of the Saints are of historical value; and fourthly in those mediaeval histories that pre-date the historical romance of Geoffrey of Monmouth or in later ones that ignore or discount his work. The picture we get from Nennius is of a *Dux Bellorum* or war lord who was leader of the combined British resistance to the incursions of the Saxons. He seems to have been of lesser nobility than many of his compatriots who provided the additional cavalry and foot-soldiers that made up the combined army. In the oldest Welsh literature and poetry he is referred to as 'Arthur the warrior.' In Welsh mediaeval literature he is sometimes depicted as fighting other Britons. In Nennius Arthur is referred to as a soldier and as the commander in battle over the kings of Britain and fighting the 'Saxons;' in one of the Lives of Gildas he is described as a 'tyrant.'

Ancient Welsh poetry.

The Four Ancient Books of Wales are the *Book of Taliesin,* the *Black Book of Carmarthen* and the *Gododdin,* which all contain poetry, and *The Red Book of Hergest* which includes some poems and also mythological tales of which the most famous are the *Four Branches of the Mabinogi,* also known as the Mabinogion in the strict sense. The term Mabinogion is also used loosely to designate other stories from the *Red Book*, and also from another manuscript known as the *White Book Mabinogion*. These books, as we know them, were written down by monks in medieval times.

The famous bards of Wales were Myrddin (or Merlin), Aneirin, Llewarch Hen and Taliesin, all apparently dating from the sixth century.

The Gododdin is a collection of verses known as the Canu Aneirin, the song or poem of Aneirin, for the Welsh have a single word *Canu* for song and spoken verse. It is an account of a battle fought at Catraeth by a warrior band sent forth by the lord of Dyn Eidyn in which all the men are killed except Aneirin who was taken prisoner and subsequently rescued. Whilst he was a prisoner he composed and sang elegies to his friends who had fallen at the Battle of Catreath. Dyn Eidin is generally identified with modern Edinburgh, but there is an alternative in Caredin, from Caer Edin (*Din Edin* in Welsh) or the Fort of Edin, on the Firth of Forth, supported by Glennie in his *Arthurian Localities*. Catreath is generally identified with modern Catterick in Yorkshire, but this seems mainly to be based on the similarity of names and the fact that Catterick is strategically placed. There are some that say Catraeth is purely a descriptive term for *cat* in Welsh signifies battle and *traeth* means a beach or a sandy tract or plain, perhaps near the Firth of Forth, but there is a poem in the *Book of Taliesin* in which Urien is called *Llyw Catraeth* or "ruler of Catraeth" implying that it is a district and more than just a sandy tract. Most of the scholars favour the site at Catterick; Ifor Williams said it is not sure if it were geographically part of Urien's kingdom of Rheged. Recently in *the Keys to Avalon,* Blake and Lloyd have questioned the accepted location of Catraeth and think it was somewhere along the North Wales coast, but it will probably take the academic establishment a long time to get round even to thinking of looking into this, especially as they have not come up with much supporting evidence and have a passion for locating everything Arthurian in North Wales. I shall say more about these writers later.

It is important to note that in the ancient world people were often better known by the name of their function or the locality of their origin than by their forename. For example, many old chronicles simply say 'the Bishop' or 'the King' or 'King Edward' and so on, without specifying which bishop, king or King Edward is intended. In a recent and important study entitled *Names from the Dawn of British legend,* Toby Griffen points out that the name Anerin or its shorter variation Neirin begins with a negative marker, 'an' or 'n,' and that this name can be interpreted as meaning "one not in the battle," in modern English the Non-combatant. The two variations would be used in verse according to the number of syllables used to make up one line. This non-combatant rôle could explain why Aneirin survived the battle and lived to sing the elegiac verses to his fallen friends.

The question now remains: what was Aneirin's rôle at the battle? He tells us that he was singing the *gwenwawd* which could mean 'holy song,' something that was first hinted at by Sir Ifor Williams. Toby Griffen concludes that Aneirin's rôle at the Battle of Catraeth was that of a Christian priest, and that he composed the verses to his fallen friends immediately after the battle and whilst still a

9

prisoner because he was singing their praises for their sal-
vation.

There remains the question of the dating and authenticity
of the *Canu Aneirin*. The oldest manuscript extant comes
from 1265 A.D.; it was copied from two sources one of
which, known as the B text shows an orthography or
spelling of considerable antiquity. This gives us evidence
that the Canu Aneirin may well originate from the time of
the Battle of Catraeth around 600 A.D. After sifting the
evidence and giving valid reasons why the text is not
simply a more recent one in which archaisms had been
deliberately inserted, Toby Griffen concludes that the
Canu Aneirin is a copy of a copy of a copy... of a late
Britonic (or Brythonic) text dating from around or soon
after 600 A.D. In an earlier work, Koch, in *When was
Welsh first Written Down,* concluded that works of literature
including *Canu Aneirin* come in part from written material
older than 750 A.D.

For our purpose, the most important point of this dating
of Canu Aneirin is that it contains the oldest sure references to the historical existence of names such as
Taliesin, Myrddin and Arthur, as well as Aneirin himself.
Aneirin is also mentioned in Nennius' *Historia Brittonum* or
British History, its source or sources possibly dating from
the eighth century, which also supports the conclusion
that the *Canu Aneirin* was composed soon after the event
of the Battle of Catraeth. Aneirin is also said to have
written a '*British History*' and a '*Life of Arthur.*' But these
works, if they really existed, have long since been lost.

The *Book of Taliesin* also includes references to Arthur and
Myrddin as well as one to Aneirin singing the *Gododdin*

about the men of Catraeth before the next day dawned. The *Book of Taliesin* as we know it is a collection of poems allegedly written by 'Taliesin.' It comes to us from a manuscript of the late thirteenth century. We can discount the claims made by J Gwynogryvn Evans that these poems belong to the twelfth century. Evans was so carried away that in one poem commonly known as 'The Spoils of Annwn' but which can be interpreted to mean 'The Treasures of Annwn' he inserted the word Saladin into the old Welsh text and then translated the whole into English calling it 'King Richard at Joppa and Acre' on the 'evidence' that Saladin was King Richard's opponent during his Crusade. Sir Ifor Williams commented that it was shameful for a scholar to treat the old Welsh texts like that. Sir Ifor concluded that there were twelve poems in the *Book of Taliesin* that were likely to be of sixth-century origin. His conclusion was based on the existence of archaic words or spellings in these poems. He said that sometimes the monk scribes would become so tired that they forgot to modernise the spellings in a poem or poems they were copying, thereby letting slip through evidence of their antiquity. More recently, Toby Griffen has pointed out that Williams was right that some of these poems were from before the twelfth century but not all of them date to the sixth. In other words Griffen thought that there had been more than one Taliesin. To understand this we must turn from the history to the legend of Taliesin, for there we find an account of the origin of his name meaning either Fine Value or Radiant Brow. Griffen proposes that the traditionally accepted name of Radiant Brow refers to a golden crown worn by the chief bard of the land. This would most likely have been a slender golden hoop, not as grand as a royal crown. Thus the first Taliesin had to earn his name through his reputation as a poet, and there was subsequently a succession of Taliesins. Perhaps the oldest poems referring closely to events and characters of the sixth century come from the first bard to be designated Taliesin, but there were successors that added to the poems that make up the Book of Taliesin. Some of the poems in that book are clearly of the twelfth century and here we may suppose that a medieval monk composing such a poem would simply ascribe it to 'Taliesin' just as others at that time would claim that a book they had written was the work of a more illustrious writer. This has been the case, for example, with Albert the Great, who no doubt wrote, but not all of the books that bear his name.

The Black Book of Carmarthen includes references to Myrddin whom we have already mentioned from the Gododdin. The reader is advised that here we have a historical Myrddin or Merlin quite different from Merlin the enchanter of Arthurian fiction. This Myrddin seems to have been a warrior who fought in the Battle of *Arfderydd,* probably in 573 A.D. That battle is said to mark the victory of the Christian Cymru over the others that were still hanging on to the old Pagan traditions. Myrddin's leader, Gwendoleu was slain in the battle. The Black Book implies that Myrddin went crazy as a result of the battle and lived wild in the forest of *Celyddon.* He lived there in terror of Rhydderch Hael. In one famous poem in the Black Book there is a dialogue between Myrddin and Taliesin which hints at a later Taliesin than the one contemporary with Arthur, otherwise it would be anachronistic.

Toby Griffen points out that Myrddin's going crazy after the battle would these days be called post-traumatic stress

12

disorder. There is a famous poem in the Black Book called the "Oh's of Myrddin," in which Myrddin addresses himself to a piglet; he also speaks to an apple tree, saying 'oh sweet apple tree, that in *Llanerch* grows.' Now *Llanerch* in Welsh means a clearing, generally a sacred clearing that was made by the founder of a monastery. This, and the presence of apple trees and pigs, implies that Myrddin had by then taken refuge in a monastery, perhaps in an out-of-the-way place, and for other reasons given by Griffen, perhaps near the sea. Aneirin, who was the earliest to mention Myrddin identifies him as the composer of a eulogy, probably for those who died at Arfderydd. There is some evidence that the name Myrddin means waterman, referring either to the water of the font or the sea, perhaps a name acquired after he had become a monk and literate.

It is probable that the historical bard Myrddin has no connection with the town of Carmarthen or Caermyrddin in Wales, for that name can simply mean the fortress by the sea. Any such association more likely belongs to the Merlin of mediaeval romance literature and legend. I must confess I felt impressed the first time I saw Merlin's Hill there, and I should not wish to say that there is no one behind the legend; it is simply that we do not have any historical evidence. Peter Roberts, who translated the Chronicle of Tysilio, of which more later, pointed out that Myrddyn could mean ten thousand men (a legion) so that Caermyrddin could mean a City of the Legions, of which there were several in Britain.

The legendary Merlin that we find in the Arthurian romances is generally regarded as fiction; the only reference I can find to a possible historical character behind this fiction is in the Annals of Clonmacnoise, where the death of one Merlyn is recorded at 546, much too early for the one that was at the Battle of Arfderydd. There is a possibility that Arthur, as were his predecessors, was advised by a Druid, perhaps one that had become Christian after his twenty or so years of training in the arts, sciences and secrets. This may be the historical character behind the fictional magician of the mediaeval romances; Peter Roberts adds a footnote to his translation of the Brut or *Chronicle of the Kings of Britain* saying that 'Arthur was rebuked by a hermit for his attachment to diviners.' We shall see later that Arthur's predecessor, mentioned as war-chief in the dark-age histories, was called in Latin *Ambrosius Aurelianus*, whom the Welsh called *Emrys*.

So far I have demonstrated that it is reasonable to accept that the ancient bards of Wales were historical personages, with the reservation that the names attributed to them were not their personal or family names but names denoting their function in life, that is to say *what* they were rather than *who* they were, and that a name such as Taliesin may have belonged to a series of chief bards of the land. Griffen points out that the name *Arturus* in Latin implies the constellation of the Great Bear whereas in the Briton tongue *Artur* means bear-man, implying bear-like attributes in an effective military leader. Arthur would have needed to rally both Romano-Britons and wild mountain Britons to fight; thus it would seem that the name was chosen for that purpose, and that it was not Arthur's original one. The name Arthur does not appear in history before this time, whereas after the time attributed by history to him, Arthur became a popular name. The Gododdin, the Book of Taliesin and the Black Book of Carmarthen all include references to Arthur, but

14

they are not to a king such as is depicted in the romances of the medieval period, but to a formidable dark-age warrior skilled in tactics and leadership, and this is the Arthur of history, of whom more in what follows.

The Dark Age Histories

Two 'histories' stand out from the so-called dark ages, for they are dark only because we know and understand so little about them. The early Celtic saints no doubt saw that period as an age of enlightenment! The two histories are the ones attributed to Gildas, and Nennius.

Gildas

Gildas wrote *De Excidio Britannia* or the *Ruin of Britain*. This is often described as a history but it is more a combination of what we would now call serious journalism with biblical-style tirades against the native British rulers, and nostalgia for the loss of Roman Britain. Gildas was a contemporary of Arthur but he did not mention him by that name. It has been suggested that the reason why Gildas did not mention him by name was because Arthur had killed his brother. Toby Griffen thought the story of Arthur killing Gildas' brother had been invented later to give a reason why Gildas did not mention him. Gildas was an early Christian holy man and he was writing his book in the manner of the Old Testament prophets implying that all the troubles of the Britons had come because they, and especially their leaders, had strayed from the true path. He mentions several leaders as tyrants, critically attributing the names of animals to them as well as giving their names.

Thus he describes Constantine, who seems to have held the Cornish peninsula, as the whelp of a filthy lioness; Aurelius Caninus who probably held an extended Powys including parts of adjacent counties such as Shropshire and Herefordshire, also as a lion whelp; Vortipor ruler of Demetia in what is now south-west Wales, as a leopard spotted with wickedness; and Maglocunus or Maelgwn of Gwynnedd as a dragon of the island. He goes even further in his sarcastic criticism of one Cuneglassus of the Stronghold of the Bear; this would appear to be Dinarth, a hillfort in North Wales, and probably not a cryptic reference to Arthur, meaning Bear-Man, as some have thought. (But Arthur may have held his court at Dinarth at one time and even given it its name; and I shall return to this later.) Gildas was thus writing a biblical-style broadside claiming that the British had been losing their lands because of the waywardness of their leaders. We shall see later that Arthur is described in some of the manuscripts of Nennius as a military leader despite his being of less noble birth than others in the British resistance force; so Gildas had no need to mention him by name, for he was out to blame the *primary chiefs* or 'kings' of Britain for the successes of the foreign invaders, and any victory he would no doubt ascribe to a chief or 'king' rather than to a battle-commander. This is similar to the view that was taken by Crawford in his account of *Arthur and His battles* which we shall consider later. Gildas mentions the battle or siege of Mons Badonicus, or mount Badon, the success of which is attributed to Arthur in the *Historia Brittonum* of Nennius, and I shall have more to say about this in a later chapter.

Gildas was the son of Caw who had several children that figured in the history and legend of what is now Wales. It has generally been believed that he was born in 'Arecluta' meaning Strathclyde, because Caradoc of Llancarvan who wrote one of his 'Lives' said that Caw of Prydyn, his father, was from Arecluta 'beyond the mountain Bannauc, which is in Albaniam' (Scotland). The land of the North British was called *Prydyn* (Pictland and neighbouring regions in Scotland, around and north of the Antonine Wall between the Clyde and the Forth) to distinguish it from the *Island of Prydein*, the land of the South British which often approximates to an extended modern Wales; *ynys* or island denoting a territory surrounded by other lands or water. *Prydein* alone can also be used to denote Britain as a whole. Gildas is then said to have been abbot of the monastery of Bangor Iscoed, south of Chester. We next find him in one of his *Lives* living as a 'hermit' on an island in the Bristol Channel where he also has his 'servants' that are captured and taken away by pirates. Then, allegedly, he turns up at Glastonbury, and we shall come back to an Arthurian episode there later. He is said to have ended his life in Brittany. The Welsh Annals record him as having gone over to Ireland in 565; and the same source records his death at 570, calling him *Gildas sapientissimus Britonus* or the wisest of the Britons. Not all historians accept the Glastonbury episode of his life. Some have thought that he wrote his famous book in Brittany, but in it he said he could not travel *overland* to Caerleon-on-Usk which implies that he was not overseas at the time of writing.

Baring–Gould and Fisher in the *Lives of the British Saints* tell us that Gildas visited St Cadoc at his monastery of Llancarfan in 528. Cadoc seized on the occasion to ask him to take charge of his monastery for him whilst he himself went into Alba [Scotland]; to this Gildas consented. There is a discrepancy between the accounts in the *Life* of Gildas and that of Caradoc. In the former it is said that Gildas undertook charge of Llancarfan for one year only. In the *Life of St Cadoc* he is represented as being absent in Alba for seven years. But Gildas had come over from Brittany and spent only seven years in this period of his life in Britain. During that time he was much associated with Cadoc in retirement in the Holmes [islands] of the Bristol Channel, so we must take the shorter time as that during which Cadoc was in Alba.

Cadoc now departed for Alba and built a monastery of stone "near the mountain Bannauc." Skene quotes Bishop Forbes as saying: "Cambuslang is dedicated to St Cadoc, and through the adjoining parish of Carmunnock runs a range of hills, called the Cathkin Hills, which separates Strathclyde from Ayreshire, and terminates in Renfrewshire. This must be the 'mountain Bannauc;' and the name is preserved in Carmunnock."

This Caer Bannauc is probably the Caer Banhed of the *Life of St Paul of Léon*. A certain Marc Conomanus was king there, and he and Paul had fallen out and the huffed saint had departed and crossed into Brittany. Now Paul was a native of Penychen, and almost certainly was acquainted with Cadoc. On quitting the territory of King Marc, he would go home to Penychen, where Cadoc would learn from him that the king of Strathclyde actually desired to have a religious foundation in his realm, and had urged Paul to take on him the ecclesiastical oversight of the people. Paul had left in a fit of spleen. Cadoc thought he saw his opportunity, and having provided a caretaker abbot for his monastery at Llancarfan during his absence, went to the realm of Marc Conomanus and took up the threads dropped by Paul and established there a monastic house.

A curious story attaches to the founding of this monastery in Scotland. Whilst digging the foundations, Cadoc came on some huge bones, and prayed that it might be revealed to him whose they were. In the night, a gigantic man appeared and told him that they belonged to his earthly remains, and that he was Caw, surnamed Prydyn, or Cawr (a giant); and that he had been a king beyond the mountain range (that is in Strathclyde) but had fallen there in battle.

What seems to be the explanation of this story is that at the request of Gildas, Cadoc sought out the burial mound of his father, Caw of Cwm Cawlwyd, who had been engaged in conflict with the Gwyddyl Ffichti or Irish Goedels and had lost his territory to them. Then as a token of friendly feeling to Gildas, Cadoc erected his monastery over the tomb of the father of that saint. The similarity of the name Caw with Cawr furnished the legend-maker with the idea that he was a giant.

On the return of Cadoc to Llancarfan, he resumed the rule over his abbey, and Gildas is said to have retired to Glastonbury; but the friends were wont during Lent to retreat to the Steep and Flat Holmes in the estuary of the Severn, for prayer and meditation, broken only by visits to each other. I remind readers that some historians have doubted whether Gildas ever was at Glastonbury. Blake and Lloyd think that the *Glastonia* that had associations with Gildas was near to Llangollen, and that the old Welsh name of that monastery was changed to Vale Crucis when it was rebuilt in stone and re-founded on the same site.

The northern origin of Gildas has been questioned recently by Blake and Lloyd in their book *Pendragon* where they say that his birthplace of Arecluta can mean Clydeside in what is now Scotland, or the Vale of Clwyd in North Wales. They say that in the *Life of St. Cadoc,* Caradoc of Llancarfan deliberately transposed a story of Caw the father of Gildas being from the land of Clwyd in Wales, to Scotland, in order to imply that his monastery had lands even in the far North. The professional hagiographers that wrote the 'Lives' of saints were commonly employed to boost the prestige of a saint in order to promote the territorial interests of a monastery, and they were generally far from honest in what they did. Caradoc was patronised by Robert of Gloucester who had his personal motives for promoting Arthuriana in relation to his own possessions and the political interests of the Anglo-Norman monarchy. The Latin name for Caw is Cauno and Blake and Lloyd have produced an inscribed stone from North Wales dating from around the sixth century with the name Cavo or Cauo on it, but this is not quite Cauno. They have also pointed out that there is a mountain called Bannog near the Clwyd as a possible alternative to Bannockburn or Carmunnock in the North, all of which approximate to the Bannauc of Caradoc's *Life of Gildas.* To accept this relocation one has to believe that Caradoc deliberately inserted the words Albaniam (Scotland) and Prydyn (the land of the North Britons, and Pictland) into his account. One would also need to know when the church at Cambuslang was first dedicated to Cadoc. Caradoc wrote both *Lives,* and the discrepancy between one year in Alba in one of the Lives and seven years in the other, I think implies that he exaggerated the time spent in Alba in the Life of Caradoc, rather than that he fabricated the entire northern episode. Most historians will continue believing in a Clydeside origin for Gildas, though I think there may well have been confusion at some time or other between Clydeside and the Vale of Clwyd, and the presence of a mountain called Bannog south of it provides serious food for thought. It all needs further investigation. Tradition ascribes twenty-four brothers to Gildas, but many of these children of Caw seem to be spurious additions. We shall see later that Caradoc of Llancarvan also describes Hueil, a brother of Gildas, as swooping down from Scotia or Scotland.

Whatever the truth of Gildas' birthplace, it is a fact that he only criticises the rulers of what is now Cornwall and Wales and not those of the North. This can be read in three ways, either he did not wish to criticise those in the North with whom he had had friendly relationships in the past, or it could mean that where he was living he had no proper information of the goings-on in the North, especially as the *Life of Caradoc* says that Caw the father of Gildas had lost his territory there; or if Blake and Scot are right, he had not been born on Clydeside.

After having mentioned the success of one Ambrosius Aurelianus in the struggle against the Saxons; Gildas goes on to say that the British success at the Battle of Badon established a lasting peace with them, but he does not mention Arthur. Some have said that Gildas was writing at Gastonbury, others in Brittany, and the truth is that we don't really know where he was at the time of writing. As I have already mentioned, his statement that he could not travel overland to Caerleon-on-Usk implies that he was not in Brittany and that he was prevented from doing so because the Britons had reverted to tribalism under nu-

21

merous petty 'kings' or rulers that were engaged in frequent warfare with one another, even during the peace
established with the Saxons after Badon.. When we look
at the next book we shall see that it deals with events over
a wider geographical area.

Nennius

The second book, attributed to Nennius, the *Historia
Brittonum* or *History of the Britons*, is generally thought to
date from early in the ninth century, although there are
those who think the first part of this work might well have
been written down in the seventh century, and the later
parts even as late as the early eleventh. In other words the
work we have bearing the name of Nennius is probably
originally a compilation of earlier written records and that
additions have been made subsequently. It is possible that
'Nennius' compiled his work from one or more now lost
sources such as a *'British History'* attributed to Rhun ap
Urien. From our point of view this is the oldest book that
mentions Arthur by name, not as a king but as being the
battle-leader of the chiefs of Britain. He could be regarded as following the Romano-British tradition of *Dux
Bellorum* or War Chief, and he probably relied greatly on
cavalry, for the chariot of the ancient Britons had by then
been abandoned in favour of the rapid deployment and
greater mobility of mounted troops. The work that we
call Nennius is perhaps best known because it describes
the locations of twelve battles fought by Arthur, but we
shall deal with these battle-sites later. Thus it is in
Nennius that we find Arthur fighting with the kings of the
Britons against the Saxons with supreme command of the
combined armies. We shall see later that not all of the
fighting was against 'Saxons.' Arthur is clearly not des-

22

cribed as a king himself, though Nennius uses the word 'kings' to describe other British leaders. The Britons had the notion of kingship but later on their chiefs took the title of *twysogion* or princes with a single overlord titled king. There are also some *Memorabilia*, of wonders and marvels of Britain, attached to Nennius; in two of these fabulous tales Arthur is described as *Arthuri militis*, once again Arthur the soldier, and not king. Richard Rowley who made the most recent translation of Nennius thought that the marvels of Britain were not part of the original work, but added later. They were already included in the editions of the early ninth century. Nennius probably wrote his book in Wales. The *Annales Cambriae* or Welsh Annals are also generally appended to Nennius; they record the British victory attributed to Arthur at the battle of Badon as in the year 516, and the battle of Camblan [Camlan] in which Arthur and Mordred fell as in the year 537.

2. MEDIAEVAL LITERATURE

Caradoc's Life of Gildas.

The Lives of many of the dark-age saints were mostly written down centuries after their time; they can seldom be relied upon as accurate sources of history, and each Life was written primarily to promote the cult of a particular saint. However, we can find fragments of alleged Arthurian history here and there, especially in those Lives that pre-date Geoffrey of Monmouth's popularisation of the Arthur of romance. For example, in the twelfth-century *Life of Gildas* by Caradoc of Llancarfan there is a comment that:

"Glastonbury was besieged by the tyrant Arthur with an innumerable host because of his wife Gwenhwyfar, whom the aforesaid evil king Melwas had violated and carried off bringing her there for safety, because of the invulnerable position's protection provided by the thickened fortifications of reeds, rivers and marshes. The war-like king had searched for the queen throughout the cycle of one year, and at last heard that she resided there. Thereupon he called up the armies of the whole of Cornwall and Devon and war was prepared between the enemies.

When the abbot of Glastonbury — attended by the clergy and Gildas the Wise — saw this, he stepped in between the contending armies, and peacefully advised his king Melwas that he should restore the kidnapped lady. And so, she who was to be restored was restored in peace and good will. When these things had been done, the two kings gave to the abbot many territories; and they came to visit the church of St. Mary to pray; the abbot sanctioning the dear fraternity in return for the peace they enjoyed and the benefits which they had bestowed and which they were about to bestow yet more plentifully. Then, reconciled, the kings left swearing reverently to obey the most venerable abbot of Glastonbury, and not to violate the holiest part or even the lands bordering on the land of its over-seer."

This account, in which Arthur is described as a tyrant, and later as a king, is quite different from the story we all know of Lancelot stealing Gwenhwyfar from Arthur in the medieval romance. It might have some historical basis but there are equally strong or stronger legends in Scotland of Arthur's wife willingly allowing Medrawd to steal her away. There are also Welsh traditions concerning Gwenwyfar's unfaithfulness and the enmity between Arthur and Medrawd. Perhaps the only history here concerns the Welsh tradition of the unfaithfulness of Arthur's wife, and has nothing to do with the geographical location at Glastonbury.

There is another episode in Caradoc's Life of Gildas that mentions a dispute between Arthur and Hueil:

"St. Gildas was the contemporary of Arthur, the king of the whole of Britain, whom he loved exceedingly, and whom he always desired to obey. Nevertheless his twenty-three brothers constantly rose up against the aforementioned rebellious king, refusing to own him as their lord; but they often routed and drove him out from forest and the battle-field. Hueil, the elder brother, an active warrior and most distinguished soldier, submitted to no king, not even to Arthur. He used to harass the latter, and provoke the greatest anger between them both. He would swoop down from Scotland, set up conflagrations, and carry spoils with victory and renown. In consequence, the king of Britain, on hearing that the high-spirited youth had done such and was doing similar things, pursued the victorious and excellent youth who, as the inhabitants used to assert and hope, was destined to become king. In the hostile pursuit and council of war held in the island of Minau, he killed the young plunderer. After that murder the victorious Arthur returned, rejoicing greatly that he had overcome his bravest enemy. Gildas, the historian of the Britons, who was staying in Ireland directing studies and preaching in the city of Armagh, heard that his brother had been slain by King Arthur. He was grieved at hearing the news, wept with lamentation, as a dear brother for a dear brother. He prayed daily for his brother's spirit; and, moreover, he used to pray for Arthur, his brother's persecutor and murderer, fulfilling the apostolic commandment, which says: 'Love those who persecute you, and do good to them that hate you.'"

There is a stone known as the Maen Huail at Ruthin in North Wales with a plaque saying that according to tradition King Arthur beheaded Huail brother of Gildas on it. This may reflect actual history, but one needs to know when the plaque was written and in what circumstances. We must be careful because of the story of Gellert's Grave relocated to Wales from Central Europe as a tourist lure. And here I digress into another one: Inland from Aberystwyth there is a tourist attraction in the form of a spectacular waterfall with three bridges crossing it, built one on top of the other. The name of the spot in Welsh is *Pont-ar-fynach* or The Bridge on the Monk's River but the English name for it is Devils' Bridge, accompanied by a legend that seems to be relocated from France, saying that an old woman made a pact with the Devil that if he would

27

build her a bridge she would give him the first soul across it. When it was finished she threw a piece of bread that sent her dog running across, saying "there's the soul you can have." The true alternative of "Monk's Bridge" would probably not have attracted many tourists there.

Caradoc of Llancarfan was a contemporary and friend of Geoffrey of Monmouth, despite which the above tale of Arthur and Hueil does not figure in Geoffrey's 'History.' This makes it an interesting episode; it depicts Arthur as being involved in the internal disputes of the British leaders, one against another. This is the side of Arthur's life that is to be found in the Welsh-language sources of Arthurian tradition, and which no doubt contain some history.

Welsh literature and poetry

The *Mabinogion* in the strict sense consists of four inter-connected mediaeval romances known as *The Four Branches of the Mabinogi* that are to be found in the *Red Book of Hergest,* but there are other mediaeval romances that are generally included along with these. There is also a similar collection of tales in a *White Book Mabinogion* that was found in a gentleman's wardrobe in Llangeitho, West Wales. A few of these Welsh romances mention Arthur, but this is seldom the Arthur of History but very much the Arthur of romance sometimes even described as the Emperor Arthur. Arthur's title of emperor is probably derived from the fact that more than one Roman general sent as *Dux Bellorum* to defend Britain revolted and as-sumed the title of *Imperator.* This term in old Welsh literature may come from this historical fact, and not directly from Geoffrey. One of these tales named *Peredur* may well be the precursor to the famous *Quest of the Grail,*

28

and we shall look at this in greater detail later. Other tales featuring Arthur include the famous *Culhwch and Olwen* and the *Dream of Rhonabwy*. Some of the Mabinogion tales seem ancient, even older than the historical Arthur, and some of them may have been reworked by monks to make them acceptable to their times. Mediaeval Welsh poetry includes the *Triads* that contain a number of references to Arthuriana. In one Triad Arthur is referred to as one of the three frivolous bards of the Island of Britain (approximately Wales plus adjacent lands). Arthur is also given three tribal thrones, in *Mynyw* (St. Davids), *Celliwig* in *Kernyw* (that most scholars regard as Cornwall; but Blake and Lloyd tentatively identify *Celliwig* with *Gelliwig* on the Lleyn Peninsula), and in *Pen Rhionydd* (the area that includes Dinarth near Penhryn Bay in North Wales). I shall refer later to other Welsh poems including *Preiddeu Annwfn* or the Spoils of Annwn, and *Gereint filius Erbin* about the Battle of Llongborth.

Geoffrey of Monmouth

In 1136 Geoffrey of Monmouth wrote his *History of the Kings of Britain*, which was there and then a great success and it is still read by many at the present time. Geoffrey claimed that he had translated into Latin a very old book written in the Welsh language, which had been given to him by Walter, Archdeacon of Oxford, and which gives a regular chronological history of the British kings from Brutus, the first king, to Cadwaladr, son of Cadwallon, and that it formed the basis of his book. He must also have read the *Historia Brittonum* and the works of Gildas and Bede. Geoffrey has been accused of having written a forgery that he then presented to the public as real history. He has been much maligned by historians, but he was

29

providing what was wanted at that time. William the Bastard had been succeeded by William Rufus who behaved like a worse 'bastard' than his father. William the First went into Wales with the express intention of killing all the male inhabitants and breeding half-Norman offspring from the women; children that might have had some notion of loyalty to a Norman regime. But the heavy chain mail of his men prevented them from pursuing the Welshmen when they ran up the hillsides and the expedition failed. His son made a similar attempt later. Clearly the new Anglo-Norman kings were prepared to use any means to obtain the loyalty and respect of their subjects. Robert of Gloucester was responsible for the promotion of a number of Arthurian translations, and no doubt some of the political motivation involved in the popularisation of Arthuriana was aimed to provide the Anglo-Norman monarchy with an illustrious past via their real or assumed Welsh ancestry. The Armoricans that had accompanied William the Bastard could also claim Welsh descent and they were forming the new English aristocracy and sorely in need of a respectable British past. I shall come back to Geoffrey and the *Brut* shortly, but first we shall look at what some of the other mediaeval historians said about Arthur, and Geoffrey:

William of Malmesbury.

William of Malmesbury was probably writing a few years before the appearance or dissemination of Geoffrey of Monmouth's portrayal of the Arthur of romance. He wrote: "When this man [Wortemer, the son of Votigern] died, the British strength decayed; their hopes becoming diminished, fled; and they would have soon perished altogether, had not Ambrosius, the sole survivor of the

Romans, who became monarch after Vortigern, quelled the presumptuous barbarians by the powerful aid of warlike Arthur. This is that Arthur, of whom the Britons fondly fable even to the present day; a man worthy to be celebrated, not by idle fictions, but in authentic history. He indeed, for a long time upheld the sinking state, and roused the broken spirit of his countrymen to war. Finally, at the siege of Mount Badon, relying on an image of the virgin which he had affixed to his armour he engaged nine hundred of the enemy single-handed, and dispersed them with incredible slaughter. On the other side, the Angles, although they underwent great vicissitudes of fortune, filled up their wavering battalions with fresh supplies of their countrymen; rushed with greater courage to the conflict, and extended themselves by degrees, as the natives retreated, over the whole island; the counsels of God, in whose hand is every change of empire, not opposing their career. But this was effected in the process of time; for while Vortigern lived, no new attempt was made against them."

Malmesbury's comment that Arthur dispatched nine hundred of the enemy at the battle of Badon 'single handed,' probably means that Arthur won that battle with none but his own men, and without the assistance of the troops of most of the other British 'kings.' I should add that it is uncertain whether the cult of the Virgin was well-developed here at that time. Thus the tale that Arthur had an image of the Virgin on his armour is likely to be a monkish interpolation, not added by William himself, but in his source. Malmesbury is generally regarded as having been the most astute and reliable of the mediaeval historians. He wrote before the time when Geoffrey's *History* became famous; but it is important to note that he is careful to separate his acceptance of Arthur as a military leader from the Arthur 'about whom the Britons fondly fable even to the present day.' We shall see that the next historian quoted fails to make this distinction.

The History of William of Newborough.

William of Newborough, who was born in 1135 or 1136, spent most of his life as a canon of Newborough — a priory of Black or Augustinian monks. He wrote a *History* which begins in 1066 and ends in 1197. In the preface to that work he writes: "For the purpose of washing out those stains from the character of the Britons, a writer in our times has started up and invented the most ridiculous fictions concerning them, and with unblushing effrontery, extols them far above the Macedonians and Romans. He is called Geoffrey [of Monmouth], surnamed Arthur, from having given, in a Latin version, the fabulous exploits of Arthur (drawn from the traditional fictions of the Britons, with additions of his own), and endeavoured to dignify them with the name of authentic history; moreover he has unscrupulously promulgated the mendacious predictions of one Merlin, as if they were genuine prophecies, corroborated by indubitable truth, to which also he has himself considerably added during the process of translating them into Latin. He further declares that this Merlin was the issue of a demon and a woman, and, as participating in his father's nature, attributes to him the most exact and extensive knowledge of futurity; whereas, we are rightly taught by reason and the holy scriptures, that devils, being excluded from the light of God, can never by meditation arrive at the cognizance of future events; though by the means of some types, more evident to them than to us, they may predict events to come rather by conjecture than by certain knowledge. Moreover, even in their conjectures, subtle though they be, they often deceive themselves as well as others; nevertheless they impose on the ignorant by their feigned divinations, and arrogate to themselves a prescience which, in truth, they do not possess. The fallacies of Merlin's prophecies are indeed evident in circumstances which are known to have transpired in the kingdom of England after the death of Geoffrey himself, who translated these follies from the British language; to which, as is truly believed he added much of his own invention...."

"....it is plain that whatever this man published of Arthur and of Merlin are mendacious fictions, invented to gratify the curiosity of the undiscerning. Moreover it is to be noted that he subsequently relates that the same Arthur was mortally wounded in battle, and that, after having disposed of his kingdom, he retired into the Island of Avallon, according to the British fables, to be cured of his wounds; not daring, through fear of the Britons to assert that he was dead — he whom these truly silly Britons declare is still to come. Of the successors of Arthur, he feigns with similar effrontery, giving them the monarchy of Britain even to the seventh generation, making those noble kings of the Angles (whom the venerable Beda declares to have been monarchs of Britain) their slaves and vassals. Therefore, let Beda, of whose wisdom and integrity none can doubt, possess our unbounded confidence, and let this fabler, with his fictions, be instantly rejected by all." [But the reader should note that Bede probably only had access to the Anglo-Saxon and continental material for his writings, and not to the Welsh literature.]

This tirade of William of Newborough represents the extreme view of Geoffrey. If one takes the view that

33

Geoffrey's book is a historical novel based on some fragments of history overlain by old tales that others have woven around Arthur's name and the whole has been then put together using Geoffrey's fertile imagination, then one can see it in a different light. It is a Romance, a Celebration that has captured the imagination of generations of readers ever since it was written. Geoffrey's Merlin as a magician has nothing to do with Myrddin the ancient bard, and Arthur's alleged exploits on the Continent do not belong to any Arthur of British history. Despite all this, if we accept Geoffrey's book not as history but as a historical novel, then we have a possible milestone of British literature. We shall see later that Geoffrey's alleged source book, the Brut, can reveal history once one goes back to the Welsh place and river-names in it and translates them correctly. Geoffrey's real misdeed appears to be that he deliberately mistranslated place-names from Welsh into Latin to suit the politics of the Anglo-Norman monarchy, and the interests of Robert of Gloucester, and I shall come back to this later.

The Chronicle of Henry of Huntingdon

Henry of Huntingdon was not simply a chronicler; he was one of the earliest mediaeval national historians of Britain, and he does not seem to have been aware of the work of Geoffrey of Monmouth, which no doubt took some time to become well known. He was probably born between 1080 and 1090. He is believed to have died soon after the accession of Henry II in 1154. He certainly accepted Arthur as a historical character, and took his information from one of several copies of Nennius that had been attributed to Gildas:

34

"In those times Arthur the mighty warrior, general of the armies and chief of the kings of Britain, was constantly victorious in his wars with the Saxons. He was the commander in twelve battles, and gained twelve victories. The first battle was fought near the mouth of the river which is called Glenus [Glenn]. The second, third, fourth and fifth battles were fought near another river which the Britons called Duglas, in the country of Cinuis: the sixth on the river called Bassas. The seventh was fought in the forest of Chelidon, which in British is called Cat Coit Celidon. The eighth battle against the barbarians was fought near the castle Guinnion, during which Arthur bore the image of St. Mary, mother of God and always virgin, on his shoulders, and by the grace of our Lord Jesus Christ and the blessed Mary his mother, the Saxons were routed the whole of that day, and many of them perished with great slaughter. The ninth battle he fought at the city Leogis [or Legionis, of the legion], which in the British tongue is called Kaerlion. The tenth he fought on the bank of a river which we call Tractiheuroit; the eleventh, on a hill which is named Brevoin, where he routed the people we call Cathbregion. The twelfth was a hard-fought battle with the Saxons on Mount Badon, in which 440 of the Britons fell by the swords of their enemies in a single day, none of their host acting in concert, and Arthur alone receiving succour from the Lord. These battles and battle-fields are described by Gildas the historian, but in our times the places are unknown, the Providence of God, we consider, having so ordered it that popular applause and flattery, and transitory glory, might be of no account. At this period there were many wars, in which sometimes the Saxons, sometimes the Britons, were victors; but the more the Saxons were defeated, the more they recruited their forces by invitations sent to the people of all the neighbouring countries."

Roger of Wendover

There were other mediaeval historians less careful and less critical than William of Malmesbury. For example Roger of Wendover, writing in the twelfth and early thirteenth century, takes the fabulous tales of Arthur as history, from his coronation as king through numerous victories and on to his expedition to Rome, following Geoffrey of Monmouth throughout. His account follows so close to the one in the *Brut* given below verbatim, that I do not reproduce it here.

The Brut
or Chronicle of the Kings of Britain
Translated from the Welsh Copy
Attributed to Tysilio.

In addition to the Latin text of the *Historia Regum Britanniae* or *History of the Kings of Britain*, we have the Welsh text of the *Chronicle of Tysilio*, which was translated into English by Peter Roberts in 1811. There is a more modern translation by Griscom done in 1929 which gives the place-names in Welsh, but the one by Roberts is suitable for our purposes, especially I have added the Welsh place-names from the Myvirian Archaiology, sometimes with modernised spellings such as "w" replacing the unfamiliar "σ." I have used the translation by Roberts because he included some notes to it that I mention elsewhere in this book. Some people have thought this could be the "old Welsh book" referred to as his source by Geoffrey of Monmouth, but many historians think this is also the work of Geoffrey, and its attribution to Tysilio is fraudulent. In other words, they think that Geoffrey produced this Welsh version after he wrote his Latin *History* as evidence for his source; but if one looks at the Welsh place-names in the Brut one can find evidence that Geoffery deliberately mis-translated them to suit the interests of his patron at that time, Robert of Gloucester. This lends support to the idea that the Brut was in fact the old Welsh Book that Geoffrey 'translated.' I shall return to this point later. The original old book in question could well have begun life at the time of Tysilio in the sixth century when it would have been little more than a list of names of old British chiefs, their descent, their battles, and maybe a few brief anecdotes, but by Geoffrey's time it could have included many interpolated or added fables, such as those that William of Malmesbury said the British were so fond of. This is particularly true of the account of Arthur's adventures abroad which seems to be an interpolated romance.

The text of the *Brut* or *Chronicle of Tysilio* that deals with Arthur is in three sections which are consecutive in the book; they can be titled *The Birth of Arthur, Arthur's British campaigns,* and *the History of Arthur and Medrod.* I reproduce in full the first two of these sections, but the third section seems to be an interpolation giving in the main an account of Arthur's fictional adventures on the continent. I have not reproduced the text of this, but merely the briefest of summaries with a comment on one item that may have some historical truth concerning relationships with the Saxons of England after Arthur's campaign in Britain.

I have kept the English-language place names given by Peter Roberts (following Geoffrey) unchanged, in parenthesis, so that the reader will be able, later, to understand what happened when Geoffrey first "translated" them from Welsh. Place-names such as London are doubtful; Blake and Lloyd say the Welsh *Llundain* had been confused with London but it should be identified with Ludlow in Shropshire, and this makes sense. Likewise other towns such as Silchester, York, Bath, Lincoln, and so on make no sense when one realizes that lowland Britain had been quickly taken over by the Saxons. I shall explain the necessary corrections in the next chapter and provide there a summary of Arthur's battles in the Brut with the corrected names of places and rivers. I give in parenthesis the names in Geoffrey's *History* followed by the abbreviation G.M. Readers should note that there are several extant manuscripts of the Chronicle of Tysilio and that the spelling of names differs in them, sometimes widely, as it does with that in G.M. When copies were made, it was usual for one monk to read out aloud whilst another one wrote; in the case of unfamiliar or foreign names, the monk reading would often pronounce badly so that when one was dealing with a copy of a copy, and so on, names given could read quite differently. Note that *Brut* comes from the French word *Bruit* meaning a report or rumour (chronicle). This title *Brut* is taken from the *Book of Basingwerke Abbey*. I also remind readers that the Merlin contemporary with Uther is from before the time of the historical bard called Myrddin or Merlin in the old Welsh poems. The Merlin of this chronicle is regarded by historians as fictitious, but I have already said that Arthur may well have had an advisor that had been trained as a Druid. In what follows I give any comments in parenthesis to identify them separately from the texts reproduced. Arthur's alleged exploits on the continent certainly do not belong to our Arthur, but they may have been erroneously ascribed to him from someone else's continental adventure. I shall come back to this later. The comments in parenthesis at the end of the first paragraph, after the *Birth of Arthur* heading, are important because Peter Roberts thought they gave evidence that Geoffrey probably did 'translate' his *Historia* from the Welsh text of this chronicle.

By way of introduction and before the Arthurian extract I give the *Epistle* of Geoffrey and also the *Introduction* because it includes a possible reference to the antiquity of the original Welsh text which if true has no doubt been embellished, interpolated and modified subsequent to the time of Tysilio:

*Prefatory Epistle from Geoffrey of Monmouth
to Robert, Earl of Gloucester.*

HAVING in the course of various readings and meditations, taken up the subject of the History of the Kings of Britain, I was much surprised to find that neither Gildas, nor Bede, though they have written copiously concerning them, have taken any notice of those kings who lived before the incarnation of Our Lord, or even of Arthur; or many more who succeeded since that event; although their actions certainly merit eternal celebrity, and are by many nations firmly retained in mind and recited from memory with pleasure. These and similar reflections had frequently occurred to me when Walter, the Archbishop of Oxford [probably Walter Calenius who has been confused with Walter Mapes] a person pre-eminent both in eloquence and his knowledge of foreign history, brought me a very old book written in the Welsh language, which gives a regular chronological history of the

British kings from Brutus the first king to Cadwaladr, the son of Cadwallon, and gives it in good language.

This book I have carefully translated into Latin, at his request, and resting content with my own simple style have not looked for pompous expressions in the stories of others. For had I loaded the page with bombastic expressions, the reader would have had more toil to understand the words, than the history itself. Favor then, Prince Robert of Gloucester, this poor effort of mine so that by your suggestions and revisal it may appear in so correct a form as to be esteemed, not the result of the feeble exertions of Geoffrey of Monmouth, but of the genius of him who is by birth son of Henry King of England; by his knowledge of the liberal arts, a man of Philosophic erudition; by his honorable military services entitled to command the field and whom Britain in these days regards a second Henry, and most sincerely congratulates herself on the acquisition.

[I have mentioned that Robert of Gloucester had motives for wanting to situate Arthur in certain locations; these included Cornwall, Lincoln, and also English and perhaps even Scottish locations to suit the claims of the Anglo-Norman monarchy. In the Epistle to the Brut Walter tells us that he had translated his original Welsh copy into Latin, and that in his old age he had translated it back into Welsh. This implies two things, first that he had given his original Welsh copy to Geoffrey of Monmouth, and second that his Latin translation had not pleased Robert of Gloucester who had probably given him the Welsh book in the first place. Robert wanted a biased or forged translation that changed the Welsh-place names into the

ones that suited his motives, and he had found a more
pliable "translator" in Geoffery.]

Introduction to the History.

BRITAIN best of Islands, formerly called *Albion,* or the
White Island, is, situated in the Western Ocean, between
Gaul and Ireland. It is in length 800 miles, in breadth 200,
and is inexhaustible in every production necessary to the
use of man. For it has mines of all kinds, the plains are
numerous and extensive, the hills high and bold, and the
soil well adapted to till, yields its fruits of every species in
their seasons. The woods abound with a variety of animals, and afford pasturage for cattle, and flowers of many
hues, from which the eager bees collect their honey. At
the bases of its mountains, that tower to the skies, are
green meads, delightfully situated, through which the pure
streams flow from their fountains in gentle, soothing
murmurs. Fish also is in abundance in the lakes and
rivers, and in the surrounding sea; and exclusive of the
southern channel, between Britain and Gaul, it has three
magnificent rivers, the Thames, Severn, and Humber, extending their branches, as it were, over it, by means
whereof the commerce of foreign countries are imported.
Formerly it could boast of twenty-eight cities, but some of
these are now deserted, and their walls in ruins, others still
remain entire, and have churches of the saints, adorned
with beautiful towers, in which God is worshipped, according to the Christian tradition, by companies of men
and women. To conclude, it is inhabited by five different
nations, Britons, Saxons, Romans, Picts, and Scots. Of
these the Britons formerly, and prior to the rest, possessed
the country from sea to sea, until by the divine vengeance,
because of their pride, they gave place to the Pictish and

Saxon invaders. In what manner and whence they came will more fully appear in what follows.

(Roberts adds that the reference above to Romans still in Britain is in some copies changed to Normans, but he thinks Romans was the original so that the copy or its source could have been written in or close to the sixth century, at the time of Tysilio, when there were still some Romans existing here as a distinct people.)

The Birth of Arthur.

....And now Octa the son of Hengist, and Ossa, declaring themselves free from their engagement to Emrys, invited the Saxons to join them, and sent both to Germany, and to Pasgen to solicit troops; and having collected a considerable force, they fell upon *Loegr* [England], and proceeded as far as *Efrawc* (York). But whilst they were assailing the town, Uther with his army came up with them, and after a severe engagement completely routed them and drove them to the mountain Dannet (the toothed mountain). For this was a lofty and craggy mountain, and had cells on its summit.* That night Uther convened a council, in which Gorlais, Earl of *Kernyw* (Cornwall) proposed that, as the night was dark and the Britons the lesser number, they should attack the Saxons by surprise. The Britons therefore did so, and having gained the top of the mountain made a great slaughter, took many prisoners, amongst whom were Octa and Ossa, and dispersed the rest.

(**Note:** *Cells – G.M. has a hazel tree; now *Celli* the original word may be a plural of *Collen*, a hazel tree, but one of the manuscripts of the *Brut* says expressly cells in

42

the rock; Peter Roberts says 'this is a proof that Geoffrey did translate.')

Uther after his victory, went to Alcluyd, made a circuit of the whole country, and established the power of the law and Justice, reducing all to obedience to them. Having thus settled everything he returned to *Llundain* (London), where he committed Octa and Ossa to prison. There also he celebrated Easter by a great festival to which he invited all the earls and barons of the kingdom, and their wives; and the hospitality of Uther and the variety of the mirthful entertainments amply gratified his guests. On this occasion, Gorlais, Earl of *Kernyw* (Cornwall) had brought with him his wife, *Eigr* (*Igerna* G.M.) daughter of *Amlawd wledic* (Amlawdd the Great) who was considered the most beautiful woman then in Britain.

When Uther beheld her he conceived a passion for her too strong to be concealed. He could not bear to be absent from her, or if he was, sent her presents of various liquors in goblets of gold, accompanied by idle messages, till at length it became known to Earl Gorlais, who in rage quitted the palace without the king's permission. Uther also, when he knew this, was violently irritated, and sent orders to Gorlais to return; because it was a high misdemeanor to quit the palace without permission. A second and a third messenger was sent with the same orders, and yet he did not return. The king then threatened to dispossess him of his property by force unless he would return. And as Gorlais, notwithstanding the threat, refused to comply, Uther set out at the head of his troops and began to ravage the property of Gorlais with fire and sword. Unable to oppose such a power in the field, Gorlais fortified two of his castles, and in one of these, called *Dindagol* (Tintagel) and situated on the sea-side, he left his wife for whom he was more anxious than for himself; and, to avoid losing all at once, went himself to the other called *Dinblot* (Tinblot or Dunod; Dimiloc, G.M.)

Uther having discovered where he was, brought his forces against the castle and attacked it incessantly for three days together, but with so little success that he lost a great part of them. It was therefore determined to divide the remainder into three bodies, and invest the castle, to reduce it by famine. And when he had been there a week, Uther sent for Ulphin (Ulfin de Ricardock, G.M.) of *Caer Gradawc* (Caer-Caradoc; Salisbury) one of his knights, and having communicated to him his passion for Eigr, asked his advice. To which Ulphin replied, that it was in vain to think of attacking the castle where she was as it was on a rock in the sea accessible only to one at a time, and that by a path which three knights might defend against the whole world. 'My advice therefore,' said he, 'is that you send for Merddyn, who by his art may assist you; and if he cannot, no one can.'

(Peter Roberts says of Uther: .....that Arthur was his son is, I think, clear from Nennius. In his explanation of the name he says Artur-*Mabute*, Britannice, *filius horribilis* Latine. Mabute is here defectively written for Mab Uthr, *the son of Uther*. Uther or Uthr signifies *terrific*.).

This being done, Merddyn said to the king: 'to attain your wishes, I must give you the form of Gorlais, I myself will assume that of Brithael (Bricel, G.M.) a favorite servant of Gorlais, and give Ulphin that of *Medaf of Dindagol* (Tindagol; Jordan, G.M.), another favorite servant of his.

44

Thus none will know but that we are Gorlais and his two servants.'

Thus disguised they set out at edge of night for *Dindagol*, (Tindagol) and having informed the porter that Gorlais was there, he admitted them, and Uther went to the bed of Eigr, where he deceitfully told her that unable to bear her absence, he had come privately away from the other castle to visit her. That night, Arthur son of Uther was won. Uther's army, during his absence, which was known to them, assailed the castle, forced Gorlais out to combat in the field, slew him, and dispersed his adherents.

This intelligence was quickly communicated to Eigr whilst Uther lay by her side, and he having heard it, said with a smile, nay I am not yet slain, but as it is, I must go and see what has passed in the garrison; so saying, he departed, and resuming his own form he returned to his troops. For the death of Gorlais he was in part grieved and in part rejoiced, and when all was quiet, he married Eigr in secret, and had by her a son and daughter, viz. Arthur and Anna.

Uther afterwards fell sick, and during his illness which was long and heavy, those who had the charge of Octa and Ossa became impatient, and having taken umbrage at Uther, set them free, and went with them to Germany. This alarmed the Britons very much as they heard that they were levying troops there, and it soon proved to be so, for they came to *Alban* (Albany) where they began to ravage and burn what they could find. At this time Uther's army was commanded by *Llew* (Lew) the son of Cynvarch, who had married Anna, Uther's daughter, and was both just and liberal; but in most of his engagements, for he had many with the Saxons, he was worsted. For his own countrymen thought him not equal to the command, and would not obey him, and hence his ill success was so frequent and so long, that the Saxons were near having the whole island in their power, and Uther was informed that his son-in-law was unable to subdue the Saxons. Enraged at what he heard, he ordered all the men of rank into his presence, and upbraided them with their remissness as to the Saxons. He then caused himself to be carried in a litter, ill as he was, at the head of his army to Verulam (St Albans?), where the Saxons were ravaging.

The report of Uther's arrival at the head of his army in a litter was turned into ridicule by Octa and Ossa, who considered *the man half dead*, as they called him, with more contempt than apprehension; and so much so, as to go into the city, and having the gates open to brave and insult Uther and his army. Uther therefore commanded his troops to invest the city, many of whom entered it, so that there ensued a great slaughter on both sides, until night. On the morrow the Saxons came into the field, and gave battle to the Britons. In this engagement Octa and Ossa were slain, and the other Saxon chiefs forced to a disgraceful flight. Then Uther, though previously it had required two strong men to turn him in his bed, raised himself into a sitting posture, and said 'The insolent traitors called me a man half dead, but the man half dead who conquers is still better than the man all alive who is conquered; and better is death with glory, than life with shame.'

After their defeat, the Saxons who escaped collected themselves together in Albany and renewed the war as before. It was Uther's wish to pursue them; but his illness increased so much upon him that he could not bear even the litter. This, the Saxons understood and having laid a plan for his destruction, sent those who were to execute it to him under the pretext of a conference. These persons having learned that Uther drank of the water of a particular well only, which was near Verulam, they caused it and the adjacent waters to be poisoned; in consequence whereof Uther himself died as did also others who afterwards drank of them, till at length, the cause having been discovered, the Britons filled up the well with earth. Uther was buried in the circle of the heroes.

The Saxons now sent to Germany for auxiliaries, and having obtained as many as a large fleet could bring over, commanded by Colgrin, the united forces seized on the country from *Hymer* (Humber) to *Penrhyn Bladdon* (the Promontory of Bulness). All the principal Britons therefore, ecclesiastics and laymen, assembled at *Caer-Vydau* (Colchester, G.M.), and resolved to make Arthur their king.

Arthur's British Campaigns.

Arthur, at the time of his coronation, was not more than fifteen years of age, yet he was unrivalled by any within the knowledge of the age in lively wit, in valour, or liberality, so that scarcely could his revenue supply his boons to his adherents; "but where the natural disposition is liberal, God will not suffer it to be destitute of the means." The chieftains therefore commanded *Duvrig* (Dubricius) Archbishop of Caerlion to crown him king, as they were in apprehension of the Saxons.

Immediately after this ceremony, Arthur collected a great force and marched to *Caer Efrawc* (York); Colgrin (William of Malmesbury says it was Cerdic and that Colgrin had been left to guard Deira) likewise having gained intelligence of this, collected an army consisting of Saxons, Scots and Picts; and gave Arthur battle on the banks of the Dulas (Douglas.) After a severe contest, victory declaring for Arthur, he drove Colgrin, and such as escaped with him, to *Caer Efrawc* (York); where he shut them in closely, and cut off all provisions from reaching them. And when Baldolf, Colgrin's brother, heard of it, he advanced at the head of six thousand men, within ten miles of *Caer Efroc* (York,) having hitherto remained on the coast and waited for Cledric (Cheldric in Geoffrey of Monmouth), a German chief to arrive with troops to assist the Saxons. His intent was to attack Arthur by night, but Arthur aware of the design, sent Cador, Earl of *Cerniw* or *Kernyw* (Cornwall) at the head of six hundred cavalry and three thousand infantry to intercept him, which he did, and routed him with great slaughter. Dispirited by this failure in his attempt to liberate his brother, Baldolf turned his thoughts to the effecting of it by stratagem, and disguised himself as a minstrel by poling his head and cutting his beard; and thus with a harp in his hand he pervaded the British army and arrived at the foot of the city wall, where he sang aloud, and being recognized by those within, they drew him up into the town by ropes, where, with his brother, he entered into a consultation as to the means of escape.

In the mean time intelligence was brought to Arthur that Cledric had arrived on the coast of Alban with six hundred ships from Germany, and had landed there. Arthur therefore withdrew from *Caer Efroc* (York) to *Llyndain* (London), and there assembled a council of his chiefs; the result whereof was an application to Howel, the son of Emyr of Llydaw (Brittany) by Arthur's sister, for

48

auxiliaries. Howel in consequence of this application came to *Northamptwn* in the land of *Lloegr* (G.M. has Hamo's Port) with fifteen thousand men at arms, to the great joy of Arthur. From thence they went to Caer-lwyd-coed, otherwise called *Caer Lincol* (Lincoln), where the Saxons were. Here a furious battle ensued, in which six thousand of the Saxons perished, either slain or drowned. Those who escaped fled to the Wood of Celyddon whither Arthur pursued them. Here a second and bloody engagement took place, and Arthur perceiving that the Saxons, under shelter of the wood, wounded his men, ordered the trees to be cut down, and interwoven with high stakes so as to form an inclosure around the Saxons. Thus inclosed, the Saxons remained three days and nights without food, so that to avoid a death by famine they surrendered and gave up to Arthur all the wealth they had, and promised him a tribute from Germany, for which they gave hostages.

But when they were fully out at sea, repenting of the conditions they had agreed to, they changed their course, landed at *Totnais* or *Tonais* (Totnes) in the land of *Lloegr* and ravaged the country as far as the *Hafren* (Severn), and from it to *Caer-Vaddau* to which they laid siege. As soon as Arthur was informed of what they had done, he ordered the hostages to be hanged immediately. And, though he was obliged to leave his nephew Howel ill at Alcluyd, amidst his enemies, he broke off the war with the Scots and Picts, and came upon the Saxons at *Caer-Vydau*; and declared that, as they had not kept their contract with him, they were to look for none from him. Dubricius, Archbishop of Caerleon, then ascended an eminence, from whence he addressed the British army, saying,

"My Christian brethren, avenge yourselves this day on the infidel Saxons for the blood of your countrymen. So, through the blessing of God, shall the pain or death you may suffer, be an expiation of your sins; and Christ, who laid down his life for his brethren, will not reject those who so offer themselves a sacrifice."

Arthur then put on a breast plate, worthy of a king; a gilt helmet, on which were the image of a fiery dragon, and another device called Prydwenn in which was a carved image of the Virgin, which Arthur usually wore when going to a perilous engagement. He also put on his sword, called Caledvwlch, *(the, hard cleft)* as it was the best in Britain, and had been made at Afallach. He also took in his hand a spear called Ron-cymmyniad, *(the spear of command;)* and when all were armed, and had received the Archbishop's blessing, they attacked and beat the enemy, and continued the slaughter till it was night, when the Saxons retreated towards a high hill, hoping to maintain a position there. The next day they were dislodged from thence, but yet continued to fight desperately. Arthur therefore, drawing his sword Caledvwlch in rage, and invoking the Virgin, rushed manfully into the midst of his enemies dealing death at every blow; nor did he cease till he had slain four hundred and seventy. The Britons, noticing his unabated prowess and ardour, joyfully summoned up all their powers to keep pace with him, and at length Colgrin and Baldolf his brother, and many thousands with them, being slain, Cledric with the remnant of his forces fled. Arthur therefore having given it in charge to *(Gattwr)* Cador, Earl of *Kernyw* (Cornwall), with ten thousand men at arms, to pursue the fugitives, took his route for Alcluyd, where, as he had been informed, the

Picts and Scots were endeavouring to dislodge Howel from the fortress.

Cador in the mean time seized on the Saxon vessels, put part of his own men on board of them, and with the other part pursued the Saxons closely, so that Cledric was slain and those who were not killed were taken and doomed to perpetual slavery. He then went to join Arthur at *Alclyt* (Alcluyd), who he found had driven the Picts to the *mor* (sea.) This being the third defeat that Arthur and Howel had given them, after which they took refuge in the island of the Lake of Llumonwy (Loch-Lomond). In this lake there are three hundred and sixty *(islands, and it receives as many)* rivers from the mountains of Prydyn, the waters whereof flow in one stream called Leven, to the sea. In each of these islands there is a large rock, and an eagle's nest on each; and when these eagles assemble on one rock and scream there, it is known that some calamity from abroad is coming on the country.

Arthur set a guard all around this lake, having had ships and boats brought thither for the purpose, so that thousands were dying there of hunger. Whilst the Scots were in this situation, Gillamori (possibly the name of a clan not a person, perhaps from Gillian-mor *the great tribe of the Firbolg)*, who was of the same race and language, came from Ireland with a fleet to their aid. Arthur therefore, leaving the Scots, attacked Gillamori, and obliged him to fly to Ireland; and having so done returned to his plan of subduing the Scots. But now the Bishops and Abbots, dressed in their vestments, came before him and on their knees begged that he would spare the lives of that people, and suffer them and their posterity to be slaves for ever, to which he assented.

Peace being thus concluded, Arthur and Howel went to view the whole lake, and having so done, Arthur said to Howel: There is a lake not far off which is more curious than this. It is twenty feet square and five deep, has four distinct kinds of fish in it, one kind at each angle, and yet no one of them ever interferes with the others. There is also a lake near the Severn, called *Llyn-lliawn*, which ebbs as the tide fills, and does not rise to the surface, notwithstanding the influx of fresh water. But when the sea ebbs it fills, and throws out mountainous waves of water from which those who face them scarcely escape with life; whereas those whose backs are to them escape, however near they be.

From hence Arthur departed for *Caer Efroc* (York), to hold his court there at Christmas, and having on his journey been much grieved to learn how the churches had been destroyed, and the clergy put to death by the Saxons, he made Eppir (Priamus G.M.) the priest of his house-hold, Archbishop of York; directed the churches to be rebuilt, and persons fit for the duties to be appointed to them, male and female, and their property to be restored.

And now Arthur gave to Arawn (Augusel G.M.) the son of Cynfarch, the territory which the Scots had occupied; to Llew (Lot G.M., most unaccountably), son of Cynfarch, the Earldom of Lindsay (Lothian in two other mss., probably correct, Londonesia G.M.) as being brother-in-law to himself, and to Gwyar, (the mother of Gwalchmai, the *amherawdr* = *imperator* or general;) and he also gave Reged to Urien, the son of Cynfarch.

And when Arthur had regulated the state of Britain, which he did better than it had ever been before, he married Gwenhwyfar, one of the most beautiful women in Britain, and daughter to Gogfran the hero. Her mother was of a noble Roman family, and she had been educated by Cador, Earl of Cornwall.

After this, Arthur prepared a fleet in order to make a descent upon Ireland the following summer. When he arrived there he found Gillamori ready to encounter him. Arthur put him and his army to flight, took Gillamori prisoner, and reduced him and his army to subjection (G.M. made this to be a conquest of *all* Ireland).

From hence Arthur took Iceland (probably the isle of *Isla* off Scotland) in his way on his return, and subdued it; and when it was reported in the other islands that Arthur was everywhere victorious, Doldav the king of the Scots, and Gwynvas, the king of Orkney, came and submitted themselves to Arthur of their own accord and promised fidelity to him and also an annual tribute. And when the winter was over, Arthur returned to Britain where for twelve years together he remained in tranquility, and, inviting to his court men of abilities and celebrity from every country, he made it splendid by their numbers. By these means his own martial glory, and that of his soldiery, their courage, their liberality of manner and conduct were so celebrated throughout the nation that no one else was to be compared to him; and every other king feared least he should attack and conquer his kingdom.

Peter Roberts expressed the opinion that *The History of Arthur and Medrawd* which forms the final episode of Arthur in the *Brut* was an interpolation based on a romance of the ninth or tenth century, and not an old chronicle of events. It deals mainly with Arthur's exploits on the continent, and if they are based on anything historical it is certainly not the Arthur we are discussing in this book. It is not included here for readers can easily find Arthurian romance literature elsewhere. There is, however, one item of interest to us, for after Arthur has defeated the Norwegians and Danes, and reached Paris, he decides to return to Caerlion-on-Usk to hold a festival-style court there. The names of the invited guests are listed, and the interesting point for us is that if we correct the mis-translation of the 'Bishop of London' to the one of Ludlow (see later) all of the British people invited are from west and north of a line drawn from Hull to Southampton, and there is a mention of uninvited guests that came as spectators. These may well have been Saxons from south-east England and this could imply that they were not the Saxons that had been fighting the Britons, but immigrants that had come over in droves after the Saxon take-over of lowland Britain, and had come into England aggressively or peacefully and then settled down on their homesteads. We shall see later that two writers, Blake and Lloyd think the Saxons that fought the Britons had probably come by ship and occupied Gwent and the lands from sea to sea down the eastern side of the Severn and the Dee. The story continues with Arthur's alleged exploits in Gaul until, just as he was about to conquer the Roman Empire, he is called back because Medrawd, whom he had left in charge of his wife

54

and kingdom, had revolted and usurped his kingdom. He returns and pursues Medrawd's army into Cornwall where they are each mortally wounded at the Battle of Camlan, near Tintagel. It is likely that this fiction was written in imitation of Maximus who revolted against Rome and had himself declared Imperator in Britain, and then went off with the flower of British youth to try to conquer Rome.

I think I should add a note here about the insistence in the Brut that the old Celtic Church had archbishops that they never had in reality. The reason for this seems to be that during the mediaeval period the British Church was still distinctive within Roman Catholicism. The mediaeval authors seem to have used the term archbishop deliberately in order to stress that the British Church had an origin with a complete hierarchy, separate from that of the Church of Rome.

3. THE BRUT, AND ARTHUR'S BATTLES.

Most scholars tend to ignore the Brut on the grounds that it was not the Welsh source-book of Geoffrey, but a fabrication. Recently, however, Blake and Scot in *the Keys to Avalon* claim to have found the keys to understanding it. They say quite rightly that *Ynys Prydein* or the Island of Britain generally means the lands of the Britons (and not Great Britain) and that the Brut therefore deals mainly with what is now Wales plus parts of the adjacent modern counties. Peter Roberts in a footnote to his translation of the Brut says that although *ynys* is commonly translated as meaning an island, it generally means a country or a province. This is not just a British notion; in Cervante's *Don Quixote* we find Sancho Panza dreaming of being governor of an island that is clearly land-locked in the middle of Spain.

Blake and Lloyd claim that Geoffrey deliberately mis-translated his old Welsh Book into Latin, and I find that the translation of the Brut by Peter Roberts suffers from Geoffrey's influence. If one corrects these mistakes and accepts that the geographical area of the Island of Britain is not Great Britain but the lands of the South Britons, the Cornish peninsula and Wales extended into Hereford-shire, up through Shropshire and Cheshire, and possibly even further north, then the Brut begins to uncover some of its probable underlying history.

When one reads the Brut one finds that it refers to the (attempted) Saxon conquest of the lands of *Ynys Prydein,* the lands of the Britons south of the region of Pictland, largely an extended Wales. Blake and Lloyd think this story came to be relocated in England, but that originally it related to Saxons landing in Gwent (*Keint*) and not Kent in the South. They also claim that Saxons landed in the north of Powys near the Dee estuary and were given lands to live in near the wall, that is to say the one attributed to Offa, and not the Antoine wall. They claim that the wall known as Offa's Dyke was built by the Roman Emperor Severus and that it is the one recorded by Gildas as stretching from sea to sea. In Nennius there is some confusion because Severus is said to have built a wall 132 miles long from sea to sea, later repaired by Carusius who added a series of forts on it. The one repaired by Carusius was the Antonine wall between the Clyde and Forth, but it is only about thirty miles long. Blake and Lloyd say that the wall attributed to Severus must be the one that was later attributed to Offa, and I add that other historians have expressed the opinion that this dyke existed before the time of Offa. The Saxons were first invited in as mercenaries by Vortigern, a king of what is now Wales plus the adjacent counties, and not a king of the whole of southern Britain. Vortigern seemed not to have much respect from his own people and needed foreign mercenaries to prop him up, but later they revolted.

This makes sense, for England even at the time of the Roman conquest was not all Welsh-speaking, for Roman pressure on the Continent had resulted in powerful tribes such as the Belgae and others coming over and establishing independent hill-fort states in the South. This means that the people in England were not all ancient Britons as our school texts imply, and there would be little possibility of there having been over-kings in what is now England. The books we have such as the Brut, Nennius and Gildas seem to be referring to kings of the Britons in an extended Wales and the South-West. Dialect studies in

England have shown that words deriving from Welsh are commonest in counties such as Lancashire, Cheshire, Leicester, Rutland and Northampton; I think this may be largely because they did not receive an influx of continentals before the Roman conquest (but they may also have absorbed fewer immigrants from the Germanic parts than did other English counties in post-Roman times.)

Now we can return to Vortigern and his Saxons. It would seem that these Saxons eventually revolted; others sailed round and up the Dee estuary; and between them they conquered all the lands from sea to sea on the eastern side of the Severn and the Dee.

One difficulty with this is that Chester remained a Briton stronghold until around 613 A.D., and there is no mention of it falling before that date. One must assume that the Saxons had confined themselves to the eastern flank of Powys south of Chester. Blake and Lloyd also make out a case for a Pictish colony having existed in Powys since around 70 A.D. I shall come back to some of this shortly. In making the above proposals, Blake and Lloyd have taken the bold step of thinking the unthinkable and then looking for the obvious. By putting forward these views, they have re-drawn the map of dark-age Britain and one has to wait and see if or how the academic establishment react to all this. When I first looked at these ideas, my thoughts were to reject them all, there and then, but on reflection I find that some, but not all of their argument 'works,' accepting that not everything in Nennius refers to *Ynys Prydein;* for there are references in it to the English regions of Essex, Sussex and Middlesex, as well as Mercia and so on. One of the problems here is that if Gwent and Kent have been confused at some stage, this does not mean that other mentions of Kent in the *Historia Brittonum* do not refer to the one in England, and so on; and whoever put the *Historia Brittonum* in the form we know it in may have been confused into thinking that Vortigern had control over the English counties mentioned. I think that where one reads in Nennius that Vortigern ceded Essex, Sussex and Middlesex to his Saxons, that the compiler of the *Historia Brittonum* is muddled and wrongly attributing events that actually happened in England to him. Furthermore, it would seem that by the time one reaches the *Northern History* in Nennius it should largely stand as written for one is by then beyond the confusion of events in the lands of the South Britons with those in England. It is possible that academic historians will simply reject all of this outright, though there could be many points worth looking into or following up, and others that may warrant modification or rejection. Interested readers can refer to *The Keys to Avalon.*

The Saxons are described in Geoffrey and also in Robert's translation of the Brut as first settling in the Isle of Thanet, but the Welsh text in the *Myvirian Archaiology* says Tanet which in Welsh mutates to Danet or Dannet meaning the Forest of Dean, and this makes sense if Vortigern is king only of the South Britons. Hengist persuades Vortigern to allow more Saxons over to defend his kingdom and Vortigern falls for his daughter. Hengist agrees to their marriage in return for the kingdom of *Keint,* now Gwent, in south-east Wales. Blake and Lloyd claim that this mis-translation in Nennius and later in the Brut and Geoffrey were the beginnings of all the confusion; and after considerable reflection I am inclined to agree with this. These authors have also identified numerous other sites in the Welsh text of the Brut such as the

60

Giant's Dance or Circle of the Heroes, in North Wales, and this makes more sense geographically than Stone-Henge ever did. They have pointed out that London from *Llundain* or *Llyndain* can be corrected to Ludlow in Shropshire, *Caer Lud* in Welsh; a town with a royal palace that became the residence of the Prince of Wales after the conquest by Edward I. No doubt it was selected for this purpose because of its previous regal importance to the Welsh. The text of the Brut where Arthur breaks off his engagement and retires to Ludlow (and not London) to take counsel makes sense, for lowland Britain seems to have been quickly taken over by the Saxons, largely without displacing the indigenous population, followed by more and more of them coming over as settlers. Likewise the imprisonment of Octa and Ossa at Ludlow makes more sense than in London. Ludlow is on the River Teme which these authors say was mistranslated from the *Temys* of the Brut as the Thames. They further make out a case that the Severn, Roman Sabrina, was known to the old Welsh as the *Hwmyr* and that only after the time of Geoffrey was it called the *Hafren*. In the Brut the *Hafren* seems to be the Dee. The *Hymer* has been mis-translated as the Humber, and *Caer Efrog* on it is not York but the old Roman town of Veraconium near Wroxeter. *Caer Efrog* is also said to be the burial place of Emperor Constantine and his burial mound is nearby at Eaton Constantine. Once again Wroxeter makes more sense in the account of Arthur's movements in the Brut. Blake and Lloyd have also tentatively identified *Caer Vyddav* (*Vydav*) as Machynlleth, the one town in Wales situated where all of the three main regions meet; that is Gwynedd, Powys, and Dyfed. Because of its location it was chosen by Owen Glyndŵr as his capital; it is the obvious place for the investiture of a chief with the over-lordship. This

61

location makes far more sense of the Brut than does Silchester. Overall, I think these proposals clear up more geographical problems than they create, but there still remain difficulties of interpretation of the geography in the *Historia Brittonum* as well as a need for verification for some of Blake and Lloyd's relocations and name changes, including the rivers called *Hymer* and *Hafren*.

Blake and Lloyd have also identified a probable Kernyw that is commonly translated as Cornwall in west Wales on the Lleyn peninsula and adjacent lands along the north of Ceredigion Bay. However, the account of Dindagol castle in the Brut says that it is surrounded by water on three sides and the entrance to it can be defended by three knights against the whole world. I think this describes Tintagel Castle in Cornwall, and nowhere else. To reject Tintagel one would have to believe that the Welsh text in the Brut had been written by someone ignorant of the original location, and who believed it must be Tintagel. One thing against the Tintagel site is that there seems to have been a dark-age monastery there in Arthurian times, and there is no clear evidence of an early fortification. The Welsh location may be right; but it is based on there being a hill-fort by the sea on the Lleyn called Castell March, which one has to assume was the castle of the famous king Mark of Cornwall; the one where Arthur was conceived. Blake and Lloyd have however, also found a farm called Gelliwig on the Lleyn Peninsula which could be the site of one of Arthur's courts, viz. *Celliwig in Kernyw*.

Arthur's battles according to the Brut:

Let us now look at Arthur's battle scenario in the Brut. It gives only five or six battles compared with the twelve or thirteen in Nennius, and this inspires confidence: Arthur is crowned, probably with the diadem of chief warrior, at Caer-Vydav (Machynlleth) and he immediately sets out with a combined army of the British chiefs to Caer-Efrog (Wroxeter,) but the Saxons hear about this and meet him on the banks of the Dulas, north of Machynlleth. After a prolonged and severe contest he drives them back to Caer Efrog (Wroxeter) where they shut themselves in and Arthur cuts off all their supplies. Colgrin's brother comes to relieve them, but Arthur sends Cador to intercept him. Then Arthur hears that Cledrig has arrived with a large force on the coast of Albany. We shall see in the next chapter that the account in Nennius says that the Saxons wasted the Orkneys, sailed round the Picts, and occupied many regions by the Wall as far as the confines of the Picts, and most historians see this as a Scottish adventure; but the theory put forward by Blake and Lloyd would interpret this as implying reinforcements sailing round and landing by the Dee where there were Saxons by the Wall of Severus, and where they claim there was a Pictish colony. Later on in the Brut, when Arthur and Howel fight in what is now Scotland, it is against Picts and Scots and not Saxons; Arthur has already conquered all the Saxons in Wales at the Battle of Badon. I am inclined to take the view that these Saxon reinforcements did in fact come round to link up with the Saxons already settled by Vortigern; and if one accepts that Vortigern was overlord of the South Britons and not Great Britain, it all makes sense especially as the account in Nennius does not specify where, beyond saying that it was in Albany by the Wall. I think we have to accept that at least the writer of the Brut used Alba as a general term for the north, either North Wales or north in what is now Scotland, as we shall see shortly.

On hearing the news of this Saxon landing in the north, Arthur withdraws to Ludlow to seek council and sends to his nephew Howel, son of Emyr who was king of Llydaw, for additional support.

Llydaw is generally identified as a name for Brittany. Blake and Lloyd, however, claim that the *Howel ap Emyr Llydaw* who comes to Arthur's aid does so from Cornwall, suggesting that Llydaw was originally a name for, or in, Cornwall, but earlier in the Brut we find Emyr described as king of Armorica, which is surely Brittany. The name of Lydaw could have migrated from Cornwall to Brittany just as did the name of Cornwall itself, as *Cournouaille*, a province in southern Armorica. The tradition of Howel is strong in Brittany. According to Albert leGrand, Hoel the First of Brittany founded an order of Knights there, called *L'Ordre de L'Ermine*, and I shall come back to this in a later chapter. Howel's name is preserved in Brittany at a town called Huelgoat or Howel's Wood, where there is a Camp Artus or Arthur's Camp; in Wales perhaps in Crickhowell near Abergavenny, and Castell Howell in Cardiganshire.

The text says that Howel came by Ship and landed at *Northamptwn* which simply means a town in the North, the text says in *Lloegr*. Sometimes Northampton is wrongly written for Southampton. I conclude that the writer of the Brut did not know where it was any more than we do, but as Howel joins Arthur following his landing it could even have been in South Wales but we have no clear supporting evidence for this. Blake and Lloyd say that Loegr was first used to describe that which is now South Wales, but that later it was identified with England.

64

Wherever Howel came from and landed, the Brut says that united (with Arthur), they go to Caer Llwytcoed situated to the north of Wrexham, where a furious battle ensued and from where the survivors fled to the wood of Celyddon where Arthur surrounds them and cuts them off from all provisions. They surrender, agree to leave and take ship to go back to where they had come from. Howel continues, perhaps by ship but we are not told, up to Alcluyd, now Dumbarton, where he is taken ill and awaits Arthur in the security of the great fortress there.

But once the Saxons are at sea they change their mind, come back, and begin to ravage the land. Arthur by then has attracted to himself is own *teilu* or war-band, and also some of his friends with their own war-bands, such as Cador of Kernyw. He breaks off his war against the Picts and Scots, and without waiting for troops from the other British kings, goes with his cavalry to meet the Saxons at *Caer Vydau* or *Vyddau* (*Vaddon* in other manuscripts, — Breidden Hill in Shropshire) and he conquers them after a siege, and takes over their lands in such a way that a lasting peace is established in the South. This is the famous Battle of Badon.

So far, the place-name system of Blake and Lloyd works, and this is as far as they take their own reconstruction of Arthur's battles in the Brut. But Arthur then takes the road north to relieve Howel at Alcluyd, who is said to be besieged by Picts and Scots. He drives the Picts to the sea (*mor*, which Peter Roberts thought was the original, and not *Moorief* or Murray as in some translations) and this would imply that they had come by ship. The Brut says that then they (the Scots) took refuge in the islands of

65

Lake *Llumonoy*. The copy of the Brut used by Peter Roberts says this lake is in Prydyn (Pictland and nearby territories) whereas the main one in the Myvirian Archaiology (and in Griscom) says Prydain (but in this case I think it simply means Britain as a whole; the term *Island* of Prydain is generally used to denote the lands of the Britons south of Prydyn, but I shall note even an exception to this, shortly.) This lake is described as having many islands in it, as being watered by many rivers, and drained by a single river called the *Llefn* or Leven. Clearly this is Loch Lomond and nowhere else, and this would imply that the Alcluyd in question is Dumbarton and not a fort by the Vale of Clwyd as Blake and Lloyd might have us believe. We are told that the people that Arthur is besieging on this lake are Scots who had probably come overland from Dalriada (Argyllshire) to attack Alcluyd, whereas the Picts had come by ship. Next the Bishops and Abbots come to plead for the Scots who are dying of starvation on the island(s) and Arthur accepts peace terms. The only place in Great Britain at that time where Scots could have had Bishops and Abbots was Dalriada (modern Argyllshire), and the whole of this episode implies that after establishing peace by conquering the Saxons that had penetrated into the Wales of that time, Arthur undertook an expedition to fight the Picts and Scots in the North.

Blake and Lloyd, in their ardour to relocate everything Arthurian in North Wales, placed Alba in Powys and Cheshire; but I think the foregoing should convince readers that Alba was a general term for the North, either in the north of Wales or in Scotland. They say that it is absurd to think of a Welsh army fighting for a city in Scotland, but Wales and Welshness did not exist then as

66

they do today. I see no reason why Arthur could not have hazarded an adventure in the North, especially as he had just conquered the Saxons in Wales, and in those days being a warrior was a way of life and good pickings or loot was a reward for adventurous travellers. I add that it would have been good pre-emptive strategy to deal with the Picts and Scots in the North before they could think of putting a fleet together and landing on the coast of North Wales. Also, if Arthur could obtain military aid by ship from Howel, likewise they could go north and provide military aid there. We shall see another reference to the North in the next paragraph. One of the dangers of wishing to locate everything Arthurian in or near Wales is that a working hypothesis can change into a dogma so that anything that does not fit into it will be rejected. I add that at least one of the ancient Welsh poems depicts Arthur with his own ship and it would not be unreasonable to conjecture that during his apparently long life he at least visited Brittany, Cornwall, Ireland and the Western Isles as well as what is now mainland Scotland.

After Arthur's battle campaign, the Brut says that he gave to 'Arawn the son of Cynfarch the territory which the Scots had occupied; to Llew, son of Cynfarch the Earldom of Lindsay... and he gave Reged to Urien, the son of Cynfarch.' In the Welsh text of the Brut in the Myvirian Archaiology *Aron ap Cynfarch* is described further on as *brenin Prydyn* or a king of the North. So again we have a clear Scottish scenario implied here. Also, some of the manuscripts of the Brut name Lothian in place of Lindsey, which again indicates a northern location, and most scholars place Rheged somewhere in the North. Ifor Williams concluded that it straddled the lands around the Solway Firth.

On the other hand Blake and Lloyd have placed Lindsey around Caer Llwytgoed in Hopedale to the north of Wrexham, and they have also proposed a location for Rheged based on it being a mutation of Rhedeg which means march, implying somewhere on the Marches of the Welsh border. They have placed it as including part of the upper Dee and extending eastwards, but I do not think that anyone *really* knows the location of Rheged.

The Brut then continues by saying that Arthur had regulated the state of *Ynys Prydain* better than it had ever been before, and then he married Gwenhwyfar. Here we have a reference to *Ynys Prydain* after Arthur's campaign in what is now Scotland as well as Wales, so I cannot agree with the idea that this term *always* denotes the lands of Wales and adjacent English counties. In this case *Ynys Prydain* clearly means the lands of all the Britons.

In the light of the proposals made by Blake and Lloyd there is a need for a new critical translation of the Brut with revised English language place-names and a sifting of the evidence to see to what extent one can recognize an original basic text separate from any later modifications by Welsh copyists or interpolators that were not familiar with the original geography. In the next chapter we shall see some evidence of Arthur fighting in the North at Edinburgh and near Stirling.

4. NENNIUS AND ARTHUR'S BATTLES.

Here is an account of Arthur and his battles as translated from the Vatican manuscript of the *Historia Brittonum*, with a few additions from other manuscripts in parenthesis:

At that time the Saxons greatly increased in Britain, both in strength and numbers. And Octa, after the death of his father Hengist, came from the northern part of the island to the kingdom of Kent, and from him have proceeded all the kings of that province, to the present period.

Then it was that the magnanimous Arthur, with all the kings and military force of Britain, fought against the Saxons. And though there were many that were nobler than him, yet he was twelve times chosen their commander, and was as often conqueror. The first battle in which he was engaged was at the mouth of the river Gleni. The second, third, fourth, and fifth, were on another river, by the Britons called Duglas [or Dubglas] in the region Linuis. The sixth on the river Bassas. The seventh in the wood Celidon, which the Britons call Cat Coit Celidon. The eighth was near Guinnion castle, where Arthur bore the image of the Holy Virgin, mother of God, upon his shield, and through the power of our Lord Jesus Christ, and the holy Mary, put the Saxons to flight, and pursued them the whole day with great slaughter. The ninth was at the City of Legion, which is called Caer Lion [Caerleon]. The tenth was on the banks of the river Trath Treuroit [or Tribruit]. The eleventh was on the mountain Breguoin [or Agned], which we call Cat Bregion. The twelfth was a most severe contest, when Arthur penetrated to the hill of

Badon. In this engagement, nine hundred and forty fell by his hand alone, no one but the Lord affording him assistance. In all these engagements the Britons were successful. For no strength can avail against the will of the Almighty.

The comment that Arthur carried an image of the Virgin on his shield is taken from the story of the battle success of the Roman emperor Constantine after he had painted the chi-rho monogram, one of the oldest Christian symbols, on his shield and those of his soldiers.

The identification of these geographical localities has posed a problem for generations of Arthurian scholars and enthusiasts. It has also been influenced by the national and regional leanings of the various authors. Thus we find locations given for these battles all over England and the West Country, and that only a few authors have given northern locations for them; even fewer for Welsh ones. John Stuart Glennie in 1867 wrote that 'there are more Arthurian place names in what is now Scotland than elsewhere in the United Kingdom,' but I would add Welsh language place names had not been studied so extensively at that time as in recent years. In 1868, W. F. Skene wrote that some of the ancient Welsh poetry found in the *Four Ancient Books of Wales* belongs to the *Gwŷr y Gogledd* or Men of the North, who lived in what is now southern Scotland, and belonged to the British tribes of the *Cymru* and spoke their language as did the people of what is now Wales. The 'devastations' caused by the Picts and Scots in the North resulted in at least some dispossessed nobles, monks and scribes seeking refuge further south in what is now Wales, and beyond to

Cornwall and Brittany, such that some of their poetry and literature could have come with them.

Crawford wrote a reasoned synthesis entitled *Arthur and His Battles,* and unlike many English writers on this subject who sited Arthur's battles all over England, he accepted that at least some of them had taken place in the North.

Crawford pointed out that Britain is divided into a lowland zone in the south and east that could be quickly overrun by invading forces, and an upland region in the north and west that would be much more difficult to conquer. In times of invasion, beginning with that of the Beaker people in the first half of the second millennium B.C. and continuing up to relatively modern times, the highlands became areas of refuge, but that as things settled down there would be an infiltration of culture from the new inhabitants of the lowland zone. During such periods those in the highland zone would show some sort of collaboration such as is implied by Arthur being described as *Dux Bellorum* or war leader of the combined tribes or groups.

Crawford points out that the highland zone was protected by a group of six linear earthworks starting from Manchester across Derbyshire to Sheffield and thence by Leeds and Aberford to Richmond and Stanwick, marked on the O.S. map of Britain in the Dark Ages. They all have relation to Roman roads and four of the six straddle them. Nico Ditch guards the roads entering Manchester (Mancunium) from the south and east. The Grey Ditch faces towards Yorkshire and Lincolnshire. The 'Roman Ridges' between Sheffield and Mexborough mark the upland frontier with regard to an approach *via* what are now

71

modern Littleborough and Doncaster. The other 'Roman' dyke running north from the Aire at Woodlesford, below Leeds, may have been the frontier of the kingdom of Elmet. The double earthworks of the Becca banks bar the passage northwards along the Great North Road. In addition, the habitable limestone uplands of Yorkshire and Lincolnshire were protected by a thick hedge of primeval forest that ran right across England to the mouth of the Severn, breached only by a few Roman roads. These natural and artificial defences of the highland zone against attack from lowland Britain probably resulted for quite some time in a settled state of affairs. It has generally been assumed that the Saxons invaded Britain and pushed the Britons back into the highland zone, but what seems more likely is that the Saxons in England, who had come there as mercenaries, revolted and quickly took over the lowland zone without displacing the native population, and invited more of their compatriots to come over as settlers. When one reads Bede he calls these settlers Saxons and pacific Angles, possibly implying that the Angles came over as peaceful immigrants, but Bede himslf was descended from them!

The end result of this process was an Anglo-Saxon England into which the indigenous Britons had been absorbed. Much of this has been confirmed from studies of the survival of Welsh words in English counties. At that time some of the population of southern Britain consisted of recent immigrants such as the Belgae that had come in the first place to get away from Roman domination on the continent.

The unity of the highland zone was destroyed circa 613 at the Battle of Chester, and the Battle of Dyrham in 577

72

had already isolated the Britons of the south-west peninsula, but at the time of Arthur that unity was still intact.

I suggest that when Arthur was chosen as Dux Bellorum or war chief, to command, as Nennius implies, the British territorial chiefs or 'kings,' perhaps even men of more noble birth, his aim was not to conquer England, but to secure peace in the Highland zone.

To return to Arthur's battles in Nennius, one cannot be absolutely certain whether all of them were fought by Arthur. It is possible that whoever wrote the *Historia Brittonum* did not know the whereabouts of some of the battles he listed. Even the *Brut* ascribes fewer battles to Arthur than does Nennius; for example it does not mention the first one on the Glen, it reduces his four battles on the river Douglas to one, and it does not mention the one on the River Bassus.

The entry in Nennius for the twelfth battle, that is the one at mount Badon states that none fell except by Arthur's hand alone. We can take this to mean that Arthur and his men fought that battle alone, whereas the other battles ascribed to him seem to have been as leader of the combined British resistance. The twelfth battle is clearly an odd one out in that list, and I shall return to this later.

Umpteen attempts have been made to fix the location of the twelve battles in Nennius, and I do not intend to revue them all, but to restrict myself to what I think is the most probable scenario in which Arthur fights the Saxons in what is now Wales and on the Saxon border where, at the Battle of Badon, he secures a lasting peace for the

South Britons for some time to come; then he fights the Picts and Scots in the North; this would explain why he is not mentioned in the Anglo-Saxon Chronicle which deals mainly with events south of the Humber and east of Wales. Then he spends most of his time living in what is now North Wales, at times perhaps involved in the in-fighting of the British chiefs there, and finally he falls at the Battle of Camlan in Mid Wales. I shall refer to Skene who wrote *Celtic Scotland* and the *Four Ancient Books of Wales*, Glennie who wrote *Arthurian Localities*, Crawford who wrote *Arthur and his Battles*, and mention the views of other writers as I go in the text.

A campaign in the North.

Let us look now at some conventional history. A Scottish historian, W. F. Skene, writing in the nineteenth century said that 'around 410 A.D. Cunedda, the British war-chief abandoned the defence of the northern wall in the region called Manau and came down with his sons to Wales from which he and his descendents expelled the Scots that had come over from Ireland and settled in the western half. This would mean that in the first place Cunedda had retreated from the northern Antonine Wall between the Firth of Forth and the Clyde to the southern or Hadrian's Wall, permitting the Picts and others to occupy the land between the two walls in what we now call Southern Scotland. Before Arthur, Gildas tells us that Ambrosius Aurelianus was successful in fighting the Saxons. The period following the success of Ambrosius is filled up in the *Historia Brittonum* with the account of twelve battles fought by Arthur. The *Historia Brittonum* records among the various bodies of Saxons who followed Hengist to Britain one led by his son Octa and his nephew Ebissa, to

74

whom he promises "regions which are in the north next to the wall they call Guaul." They arrive with forty ships and after ravaging the Orkneys and circumnavigating the Picts, they occupy "many regions up to the border of the Picts." The Harleian manuscript of Nennius inserts the words "ultra Frenessicum mare" — beyond the Freisian sea — to which the Durham manuscript adds "which is between us and the Scots," indicating that a settlement beyond the Firth of Forth is meant. This is very probable, but the regions next to the wall, as far as the borders of the Picts, can mean nothing but the districts lying between the Fourth and the Clyde, through which the northern wall passes, as far as the river Forth, which formed at all times the southern boundary of the kingdom of the Picts. These regions are nearly equivalent to the modern counties of Stirling and Dumbarton. Traditions connected with this war invariably designate Octa and Ebissa, or Eossa as they termed him, and their successors, as Arthur's opponents.'

Thus in the North we find the region between the two walls overrun largely by Picts, but that there were perhaps Saxons who could have been there since Roman times when they were employed as mercenaries. Further to the north-west there was a colony of Scots from Ireland in Dalriada which approximates to modern Argyllshire; they also may have had expansionist ambitions, and more Irish could come over by ship if there were good pickings to be had. The poorer British people of the north may have stayed in place and found themselves with new masters, but there must have been at least some migration of refugees including the land-owners, warriors and the educated classes southwards through Cumbria to Wales and beyond. Therefore the next theatre of military action could well have been the organising of an attempt to recover the territories in the North lost to the Picts and Scots; and no doubt the British refugee aristocrats were doing their best to persuade the remaining British chieftains in the South to form a military coalition and send an expedition northwards. This takes us to the time when Arthur was chosen as *Dux Bellorum* or battle-chief.

Skene proposed that Arthur advanced through friendly country up the west of Britain, because in the east Bernicia was already strongly occupied by bodies of Angles. On his way he would travel through Cheshire and Lancashire and on to Carlisle and up to what are now the Scottish lowlands.

Battle sites in Wales

This takes us from the conventional view of history to a recent and controversial one. I have already mentioned that Blake and Lloyd, in *Pendragon: the Definitive Account of the Origins of Arthur,* have identified localities for many of Arthur's battles in the region of Wales. On the present basis of conventional history none of these could have been against the Saxons and their allies, but these authors make out a case for Saxons coming into Wales not overland by westward encroachment but by ship, invited to settle there by Vortigern.

If one goes along with the idea of a Saxon sea-borne invasion of the region of Wales, and that Saxons had occupied a coast-to-coast strip on the eastern fringe of the land of the South Britons, and were penetrating westwards; then some of the sites in Wales may well have some meaning. The sites identified by Blake and Lloyd

76

are (1) by the Roman road near the river called Nant y Gleiniant north of Llanidloes; (2-5) the River Dulas in the Welsh Lake District near Machynlleth; (6) perhaps on the Dee estuary near Basingwerk; (7) probably a forest near Denbigh; (8) Castellum Guinnion as Kayeguinnion in Denbighshire or Carreg Gwinnion in the Berwyn Mountains and near the border; (9) probably Chester was the Urbs Legiones in question; (10) the River Tribruit. Blake and Lloyd did not propose a location for this one, but I add that there is a river in North Wales called the *Try-weryn* which falls into the Dee near Bala; this name is very similar to the combination *Try-wruid*, but I have not seen where it falls into the Dee nor whether there is a plain or sandy tract there; (11) not far from Chester, north of Whitchurch there is a hillfort called the Maiden's Tower (Maiden Castle, which could be an alternative name for Mons Agned;) and the name Agden occurs nearby; (12) the last battle at Breidden; see below.

Those who take the conventional view of the Saxon invasion of Britain have to assume that Arthur fought a campaign beyond the borders of Wales. Blake and Lloyd have, however, drawn attention to a site near Welshpool on the border of Wales that is a serious candidate for the famous Battle of Badon. These authors point out that Gildas gives us no clue as to the location of this battle, but a Welsh romance called *The Dream of Rhonabwy* gives the route taken by Arthur to *Caer Faddon* or Badon and that it was by the *Rhyd-y-Groes* or the Ford by the Cross, on the Severn. This was identified by Egerton Phillimore and is quoted in the *Welsh Classical Dictionary* as a ford at Buttington, east of Welshpool. The story implies that this is not far from Badon, within half-a-day's march, and a spur of the Long Mountain was first suggested, but Blake

77

and Lloyd propose a hill a few miles further north that is called Breidden on the O.S. maps. Despite the risk of taking geographical locations from a mediaeval romance, the writer of which may have been influenced by post-Galfredian ideas, I think this site is worth taking seriously as a little of the fire behind the smoke; it is perhaps the most convincing proposal to date for the location of this battle. This location could explain why Gildas did not know where it was. Somewhat disconcertingly, the Welsh Annals record a 'second Battle of Badon' at 675 A.D. and this seems to correspond with an entry in the Anglo-Saxon Chronicle for a Battle of Bedan or *Beiden heafod*, the spelling of which can be compared with the name of the hill of Breidden above.

I shall comment on Blake and Lloyd's views about the battle of Camlan later, but for the moment I would digress to add that they have done some excellent work in identifying Arthurian localities in Wales, and their associations with Arthur and his contemporaries mentioned in the Welsh Triads and other literature. These authors appear to see Arthur as a leader of a war band in Wales, and never anywhere else. Peter Roberts in a footnote to his translation of the *Brut* says that Mr Jones of *Gelly Lyfdy* quotes the following from the *San-Greal*: "Arthur, when he had completed the conquest of the Saxons, made North Wales his principal residence." I take this reference seriously, and It fits in well with the number of Arthurian localities identified by Blake and Lloyd; localities that they have related with the in-fighting of the old Welsh literature. But if we are not going to re-write Nennius and the Brut, I think we must allow the possibility that Arthur fought also beyond the borders of what is now Wales, as well as within them, and at the Battle of Badon that was

78

probably on the Welsh/Saxon border at that time. In the light of at least some of the proposals put forward by Blake and Lloyd there is clearly a need for a revision of Nennius and an attempt to sort out the geography in relation to the muddling of Great Britain and *Ynys Prydein* or the lands of the Britons.

Blake and Lloyd say that there is little evidence left of the lands of the Britons in the North, and they therefore dismiss the Northern Cymry as an academic legend. This lack of evidence is understandable because the great period of scribal activity in the monasteries was in the twelfth century and beyond, at a time when the Britonic lands of Cheshire, Lancashire, West Yorkshire, the Lake District and the whole of Strathclyde-Cumbria to Dumbarton had lost their independence and their people found themselves dominated by and absorbed into 'foreign' cultures and languages. Only in Wales was the language and literature of the Britons preserved and nurtured to any extent. This was because the Welsh were the only sizeable emerging British nation that remained independent long enough. Welsh literature is thus largely about the geographical area of the South Britons which coincides with modern Wales plus the adjacent counties, and with the possible inclusion of some items brought down by the old *Gwŷr y Gogledd* or Men of the North. Some of the Men of the North are described as *o dir Manau* meaning from the land of Manau Gododdin. With reference to this lost land, Skene says that after the kingdom of the Picts fell to the one of the Scots in 844 A.D., all the old land-marker names were changed and the memory of Manau there was lost forever. The name is retained, however, in Clackmannan.

The situation is further complicated because any stories based on northern traditions that were used as a basis for writing romance literature in mediaeval Wales would tend to be given a Welsh geographical context, for the authors would long since have forgotten about the old North. Arthur's final battle of Camlan is not included in the list of twelve battles in the *Historia Brittonum*, and I think there are good reasons for locating it in Wales.

One could go on listing umpteen other proposals for Arthur's battle sites all over Britain, but I think the foregoing gives us enough detail and I summarise them as follows, with comments from Crawford and especially Jackson's useful discussion of them in *Once Again Arthur's Battles*:

A summary of the battle-sites.

1. *In ostium fluminis quod dicitur Glein [gleini]* or the mouth of the River Glen. Most historians think the first site on the River Glen[i] has never been satisfactorily identified, and we cannot be sure if it were one of Arthur's battles.

2-5. The second, third, fourth and fifth battles were *super aliud flumen quod dicitur Dubglas, et est in regione Linnuis;* on the river Dulas or Douglas in the region Linuis. Sites proposed for the River Douglas in the North include two of the rivers that drain into Loch Lomond, one in Northumberland, and one near Wigan. Jackson, referring to the first two of these only, says that it is rational to agree with Crawford who opted to support none of the proposed sites. Neither of these authors even mentioned the sites by the Lancashire Douglas at Wigan that are supported by powerful legends there that tell of the river being crimsoned with blood to the sea, but which do not have a very

80

good claim to be in Linuis, for the only lake in West Lancashire is in a separate region north of the Ribble estuary; the mere at Marton near Blackpool. When we come to the Welsh Dulas (Douglas) to the north of Machynlleth we find that it is in a Linuis, the Welsh Lake District, with Llyn Mwyngil (Lake Tal-y-llyn) close by on the west, Llyn Tegid (Lake Bala) to the north and Llyn Efwnwy (Lake Vyrnwy) to the north-east. It would seem that the writer of the *Historia Brittonum* knew that there were many rivers called Dulas in Wales and to be specific he added the words in the region of Linuis (implying the Lake District of Wales). I think this is the most likely candidate for this battle or battles.

6. *Super flumen quod vocatur Bassas,* the sixth battle was on the river called Bassas. Most commentators say there has never been a satisfactory proposal for a river called Bassus, and I agree. Whitaker suggested Bashall Brook near Clitheroe but I doubt this. Once again we do not know if this were a battle fought by Arthur.

7. The seventh battle was *in Silva Celidonis, id est Cat Coit Celidon,* in the Caledonian Forest; that is Cat Coed Celyddon. Most commentators have thought the seventh battle in the forest of Celyddon refers to Scotland, possibly Etterick Forest. Translating Celyddon into the Latin form Caledonian has had the effect of convincing everyone that it was in Scotland when in fact it might be elsewhere. I am inclined to support a site in or near what is now North Wales, but I must add that the term forest of Celyddon may be a general, rather than a specific one, and the forest in which Merlin the bard ended up may not necessarily be the same one.

81

8. The eighth battle *in Castello Guinnion* or the fortress of Gwynion is probably in a Roman fort in the North. Jackson makes no clear proposal for this site. An alternative is Caeugwynion on the Welsh Border. We don't know for certain if this represents one of Arthur's battles at all, and no one really seems to know where it is.

9. The ninth battle was *in urbe Legionis,* a city of the legions. Crawford thought this could only mean Chester which fell later to the Saxons *circa* 613 in a crushing defeat for the British, but possibly here we have an Arthurian battle fought against an earlier unsuccessful attempt by the Saxons to isolate the North Britons from those in the South. There is certainly no historical evidence of any attempt to drive in the wedge between the North Britons and those of the South by taking Chester before *circa* A.D. 613. As an alternative, Skene gives Dumbarton as the city of the Legion and he gives plausible linguistic reasons in support of it as the 'town on the Leven.' Here is his argument verbatim:

'The ninth battle was in the city of "Leogis" according to the Vatican text, "Legionis" according to the Harleian one. The former adds "which the British call Kairlium." It seems unlikely that a battle could have been fought at this time with the Saxons either at Caerleon on the Usk or Caerleon on the Dee, which is Chester; and these towns Nennius terms in his list not "Kaerlium" or "Kaerlion," but "Kaer Legion." It is more probably some town in the North, and the "Memorabilia" of Nennius will afford some indication of the town intended. The first of his Memorabilia is "Stagnum Lumonoy," or Loch Lomond, and he adds "there is but one river flowing from there to the sea, which they call Ileum" — that is the Leven. The

82

Irish Nennius gives the name correctly, Leamhuin, and the Ballamote text gives the name of the town, Cathraig in Leomhan (for Leamhan), the town on the Leven. This was Dumbarton; and the identification is confirmed by the *Brut* which places one of Arthur's battles at Alclyd, the old name for Dumbarton; while Arthur's name has been preserved in a parliamentary record of David II, in 1367, which denominates Dumbarton *Castrum Arthuri.*'

Jackson's comment was that the balance of probability was in favour of Chester, but he seems to imply that this was the famous Battle of Chester of 613 that has been anachronistically attributed to Arthur. I support the site at Dumbarton because the Brut begins to make sense now that the Welsh place-names in it have been re-translated.

10. The tenth battle was by the river called *Trbruit, Traeth Tryfrwyd* or *Trahtreuroit* or *Tractheuroit.* Crawford thought it was in the North, in the region of the Gododdin. Skene said that 'the tenth battle was "upon the shore (or bank) of the river called *Treurit.*" There is much variety in the readings of this name... but the original Cymric name is given in two poems in the Black Book of Carmarthen; it is in one *"Trywruid,"* and in the other *"Tratheu Trywruid."* ... *"Trathau"* implies a sea-shore or sandy beach, and can only be applicable to a river having an estuary. An old description of Scotland, written in 1165 by one familiar with Welsh names, says the river which divides "the English and Scottish kingdoms and flows close to the town of Strivilin was called *Froch* by the Scots, and *Werid* by the British." (*Chronicle of the Picts and Scots,* p. 136.) This Welsh name for the Forth at Stirling has disappeared, but it closely resembles the last part of Nennius' name, and the difference between *"wruid,"* the last part of the name "Trywruid," and *"Werid"* is trifling… If by the *"tratheu Try-wruid"* the Links of Forth are meant, and Stirling was the scene of the Battle, Arthur's name is also connected with it by tradition, for William of Worcester, in his *Itinerary*, says that at one time King Arthur kept his round table in Stirling Castle.' Blake and Lloyd tentatively put this battle on a beach in North Wales, but along with Crawford and Skene I support the Scottish location.

11. The eleventh battle was fought on *monte qui dicitur Agned*, the hill they call Agned. Skene says that *'Mynyd Agned*, is Edinburgh, and here too the name is preserved in *Sedes Arthuri* or Arthur's Seat. This Battle seems not to have been fought against the Saxons, for in some of the manuscripts we find added: *"Cathregonnum,"* or "against those we call *Cathbregion.*" They were probably Picts.' Blake and Lloyd give Maiden Castle as a possible site for Mons Agned near Whitchurch; if Skene's argument below does not convince, then this is an alternative.

Crawford accepts the idea that some of the battles would have been fought in the North probably in Strathclyde, but he specially questions Skene's identification of *Mynydd Agned* with Edinburgh stating that he got it from Geoffrey of Monmouth and that is why he did not give any explanations or reasons for it. John of Fordun writing in the fourteenth century said that Agned was an old name for Edinburgh. Fordun followed Geoffrey of Monmouth, but not uncritically and at times he even said Geoffrey was wrong when he had other evidence. Crawford's criticism was based on Skene's *Celtic Scotland* and not taken from Glennie's Arthurian Localities which quotes Skene's reasons for describing *Mynydd Agned* as "the painted mount, which seems to be clearly identified with

84

Edinburgh the southern stronghold of the Picts; against whom, under the name of Cathbregion, '*contra illos que nos Cathbregyon appelamus*,' (against those whom we call Cathbregion) and not against the Saxons this eleventh battle would appear to have been fought.." Henry of Huntingdon quoting from his version of Nennius in the twelfth century says "the eleventh battle was fought at *Brevoin*," which could be a corruption of Bregion, and that the opponents were "the people we call *Cathbregion*." Glennie, quoting Skene adds "that it may be noted that the words which form the root of the epithets *Cath Bregion* and *Brythwr* [Pict] are *Brith*, forming the feminine *Braith*, Diversicolour, Maculosus, and *Brych* — the equivalent in Cymric of the Gaelic *Braec* — Macula [spotted]. This refers to the name *Picti*, or painted; and *Agned* probably comes from an obsolete word, *agneaw*, to paint, *agneaid*, painted." I have failed to find these words in the old glossaries. In a poem referring to Arthur the *Guledig* (war leader) in the *Black Book of Carmarthen*, we read—

'In Mynyd Eiddyn
He contended with Cynvyn
By the hundred there they fell,
There they fell by the hundred,
Before the accomplished Bedwyr.
On the strands of Trwyruid,' etc."

To some extent this at least helps to confirm that Arthur did fight at Edinburgh, whether it were Mons Agned or not, and also on the 'strands of *Trwryuid*' which is the *Tribruit* of the tenth battle. Henry of Huntingdon writes of "the people we call *Cathbregion*," and Skene quotes from an old poem in the Book of Taliesin where there is a mention of "*y Cath Vreith* or the *Cathbreith* of a strange language," implying the Picts who did not speak the Brythonic tongue; but no one is certain as to what exactly was their language, and opinions vary even as to whether it were a form of Gaelic or Brythonic.

The word *Cathbregion* seems to refer to a people in some of the copies of Nennius, including the one used by Henry of Huntingdon in the twelfth century. On the other hand Kenneth Jackson tells us that in the Vatican rescension of Nennius made in the year 944 there is no mention of *Mynydd Agned* at all, in contrast to the account in Henry of Huntingdon. There is no reference to a people in this case but to a battle on the hill, namely '*Breguoin* or *Breuoin* …. That we call *cat Bregion*.' Jackson has identified this as the Battle of the Uplands and he tentatively places it with a battle in one of the poems of the Book of Taliesin called in English the Battle of the Huts (or Cells) of Brewyn that could be the ruined Roman fort of Bremenium near High Rochester on the Scottish border. This, however, was a battle fought by Urien of Rheged, and not by Arthur.

12. Before discussing the twelfth battle *in monte Badonis* or Badon Hill, which is evidently the blockade or siege of Badon Hill of Gildas, we need to spend some little time looking at the eleventh and twelfth battles together as we find them in the *Historia Brittonum*. Mommsen, who compared the numerous manuscripts of Nennius, selected eleven that he thought were worthy of prime consideration for the study of the Britons. Two of these, the Irish ones, only name ten battles, omit the eleventh and give the twelfth without a name. It would seem that the Irish translator thought there was some confusion in these last two items in Nennius. In the British Museum there are two manuscripts, a Harleian one (no. 3859, the one that is commonly translated) and a Cottonian one; both of these contain:

> The eleventh battle on the mountain called *Agned*.
> The twelfth on Mount Badon.

There is no mention of *Bregion* – *Breguoin* etc., as in the following manuscripts; perhaps it has been dropped to provide an easy read and avoid the problem of two possible battles listed as one.

There are two manuscripts, the Vatican and Paris ones collectively named the Vatican Rescension that have the wording:

> The eleventh is named *Breguoin*, "which we call *Cat Bregion*." (*Breuoin* in the Paris mss)
> The twelfth on Mount Badon

And finally there are the remaining six manuscripts that have:

> The eleventh on the mountain called *Agned Cat Bregomion*.
> The twelfth on Mount Badon.

I have already pointed out the possible relationship of *Cathbregion* or similar as a possible name for the Picts, and Jackson's attempt to identify this battle with the battle of the cells of Brewyn attributed to Urien in the *Book of Taliesin*. The Berwyn Mountains on the Welsh border have also been proposed as a location for this battle. If the wording in Henry of Huntingdon is right, then I support Edinburgh as the painted Mountain and the people that are called Cathbregion as the Picts; with the possibility that two battles are included in item eleven of the list.

But we have now to consider another possibility. This is that the twelfth battle at Monte Badonis or Badon Hill was not on the original list of twelve battles included in the sources of Nennius. This battle is an odd one out because it seems to have been fought by Arthur alone and not as commander of a coalition of British troops. In Nennius we find it stated that Arthur was chosen twelve times to be the commander of the combined forces, so we can say that a battle fought by Arthur (and his men) alone did not belong to the original list of twelve. The variations in the eleven manuscripts selected by Mommsen may imply that whoever compiled Nennius had a list of twelve battles, of which the eleventh was *Agned* and the twelfth *Cat Bregion* or similar, probably as a place, possibly against a people called *Cathbregion*. Perhaps Nennius was convinced that the Battle of Badon, so praised by Gildas, was attributable to Arthur, and he therefore squeezed battles eleven and twelve of his original list into a single entry, number eleven, to make room for Badon as the last and crowning victory of the campaign. Back in 1938, Wade-Evans in his *Nennius's History of the Britons* put forward a similar view. The twelfth battle of Mount Badon has commonly been sited in England, at or near to Bath. Some have said this was too far west for a contest with the Saxons at that time. Loth in *Nennius et L'Historia Brittonum* expressed the opinion that neither Gildas nor Nennius had any more idea than we have of the location of Badon Hill. The site proposed of Breidden Hill near Welshpool by Blake and Lloyd is well worth serious consideration, being on the border, and it is strategically placed for a show-down with the Saxons who seem to have occupied the western fringes of the lands of the South Britons. I support this site as probably the best one proposed to date; it is on the eastern side of the Severn, a few miles upstream from the ford at Buttington which is on the northern outskirt of Welshpool. The Welsh Annals in Nennius list it at 516 A.D, but we shall see presently that it could have been earlier.

We shall see later when we examine the question of the existence of Arthur that Padel thought the Battle of Badon was implied by Gildas as a victory of Ambrosius Aurelianus, and therefore not attributable to Arthur; but there remains another possibility, for William of Malmesbury wrote of the invasion by foreigners: "had not Ambrosius, the sole survivor of the Romans, who became monarch after Vortigern, quelled the presumptuous barbarians by the powerful aid of warlike Arthur."

If Blake and Lloyd are right in their choice of Breidden Hill, a fight with the Saxons along the eastern fringe of the South Britons would probably have been too far west for it to have been recorded in the Anglo-Saxon Chronicle.

Whatever the truth, if Arthur eventually fought beyond the border of what is now Wales, it is certainly reasonable to assume that his campaign would involve securing the principal fortresses of Lowland Scotland, Edinburgh, Dumbarton and Stirling, and he would be fighting mostly Picts and Scots.

One of the problems with all this is the chronology of the Annales Cambriae and the dating of Gildas. In the Welsh

Annals the Battle of Badon is in the year 516, and Gildas said he was born in the year of that battle and that he was writing *De excidio*, the *Ruin of Britain*, forty-four years later, which would be 560 A.D. Here there is a problem of dating because in the *Ruin*, Gildas switches from the past tense to the present when speaking of certain kings of the Britons who must have been alive when he was writing; one of them was Maelgwn Gwynedd. Now Maelgwn died of the plague in 547. Skene spotted this discrepancy in the nineteenth century, but he was wrong in supposing the date of Maelgwn's death was recorded too early in the Welsh Annals. The plague epidemic began in the east around 542 and it might well have reached Britain by 547. Reno tells us that Maelgwn's death from the yellow plague is confirmed by *De vita sancti Teiliavi*, the Life of St. Teilo. To sort this out, Frank Reno points out that some of the old dates are from the time of the incarnation of Jesus, others are from the crucifixion, a difference of 33 years. In addition there have been changes in the calendar. He points out that dates involving the 19-year Easter cycles, nineteen years being a lunar cycle, were sometimes re-ported wrongly by 19 years. In *Arthur's Britain* Alcock points out that this could have happened at a time when a monk was copying from an entry referring to Badon in a particular cycle, with no further indication of date, into one involving a larger time span; a mis-identification of the lunar cycle would give an error of nineteen years. Even now we sometimes have to think twice to remember that events in say the fourteenth century are in the thirteen hundreds and not the fourteen hundreds, and so on. Reno says that if the 19-year lunar adaptation for the date of the Battle of Badon is accepted its date can be corrected to 487, and thereby also the birth of Gildas. As Gildas says he was writing forty four years later, his book

90

is then dated at 541, whilst Maelgwn was still alive. Another somewhat disconcerting entry in the Welsh Annals is that of a second Battle of Badon in 665. Wade-Evans thought this was the real date of the famous Battle of Badon and that Gildas thereby belonged to the seventh and not the sixth century; interesting as this suggestion might be it has to be dismissed as it does not fit the chronology established with the reign of Maelgwn, and other details of a similar nature, such as a letter twice mentioning Gildas by name from St Columbanus to St Gregory the Great dated, according to Hugh Williams, between 595 and 600.

If one looks at the considerable literature dealing with Arthurian localities one finds the sites proposed often seem to be biased by the nationality of the author. It is perhaps for this reason that the Welsh Camlan that we shall discuss later has not been noticed, and the Scottish and northern locations of battle-sites have been ignored by many English writers. What English writer south of Manchester would support any serious theory of Arthur at Wigan, a town with a 'pier' that was the butt of music-hall comedians? I remind readers that R. G. Collingwood, a reputable historian, placed all of Arthur's Battles in the south-east, around Sussex, and he had no difficulty in finding sites to suit the names in Nennius. Collingwood based his fixed idea on the fact that the introduction to Arthur's battles in Nennius, gives the impression that Arthur may have been fighting the men of Kent. Blake and Lloyd make sense out of this by claiming that it was Gwent (Keint) and not Kent that Nennius may have mistranslated from the Welsh of one of his probable sources, a history by Rhun son of Urien.

91

Thinking up these scenarios is not factual history, it is story-telling and at best it is reasoned conjecture, but people seem to enjoy it as do those that re-enact ancient battles. Insofar as I have a personal opinion, it is that Arthur fought a successful campaign in what is now Wales that ended up with the Saxons and their allies being driven out of lands they had occupied down the eastern fringe, and then he had an adventure in the North, followed by a settled period in Wales where he eventually fought his last battle.

I leave the last words on this topic to Henry of Huntingdon and W. F. Skene. Huntingdon wrote of these battle-sites that "in our days the places are unknown." Skene concluded with "in thus endeavouring to identify the localities of those events connected with the name... of Arthur, I do not mean to say that it is all to be accepted as literal history, but as a legendary account of events which had assumed that shape as early as the seventh century, when the text of the *Historia Brittonum* was first put together, and which are commemorated in local tradition."

5. THE BATTLE OF LLONGBORTH.

There is a battle poem called *Geraint fil Erbin* (Geraint ab Erbin) in the Black Book of Carmarthen in which Arthur is mentioned. It is about the Battle of Llongborth. The mediaeval Welsh text in the Black Book of Carmarthen says:

> *En llogporth ŷ gueleife. ŷ Arthur*
> *Guir deur kŷmŷnint a dur.*

> At Llongborth didn't I see Arthur's
> Brave men fighting with steel;

Scholars have generally located this battle near Langport in Somerset. Gereint can be identified as the last king of Dumnonia, under his Latinized name of Geruntius. He was fighting against the westward advance of the 'Saxons' some of whom by that time had hybrid German/Briton names indicating that they had inter-married with what remained of the old British aristocracy. This poem is about a disaster in which Gereint was killed. Historians date it to around 710 A.D. The mention of Arthur or his men is therefore anachronistic if taken literally. Those that support this location say that the poet was implying that Geraint's men fought like Arthur's men. To accept this one has to believe that the reference is to Arthur and his men in spirit and not the flesh, and that Langport is anglicised from Llongborth, meaning the port of the ships.

In 1740 Theophilus Evans tried to identify Llongborth with Lamport near Tresaith in West Wales, and this theory has been revived recently by Blake and Lloyd in an attempt to relocate another piece of Arthuriana in Wales. In support of this Evans said there is a "place nearby commonly called *Maesglas* but which used to be called *Maes-y-llâs* (the Field of the Killing) or *Maes Galanas*" (the Field of the Massacre,) but another author, D. Prys Williams, writing in 1905, said that the old name of *Maes Glas* was *Karn-y-Bettws Gereint* (cairn or tumulus of the oratory of Gereint). *Maes Glas* itself simply means the Green Field, so these writers are implying that it is a contraction of an older name. Williams adds that there was a field there called *Clun yr Aur* (the Field of Gold) where treasure buried before the battle was lost because the three men entrusted to hide it were all killed in the battle. There is a *Beddgeraint* or Geraint's grave some miles inland to the south east of Tresaith, near Brongest. According to the *Welsh Classical Dictionary* it is wrongly named on the O.S. map as *Troedyraur*. Cardigan Castle some miles further south was built around 1090 A.D., before which there appears to have been a fort of a Viking settler, and earlier still there was one called *Din Gereint* [the fortified house of Gereint] all on or near to the same site.

All of this implies that there was a Geraint in West Wales, but he does not seem to be the one of the Battle of Llongborth, for the *Lam* of Lamport is generally a degeneration of *Llan*, meaning a clearing, often a sacred one. Llongborth means the port or harbour of the ships, or perhaps where they built ships. The new O.S. map names the place near Tresaith correctly as *Llanborth* meaning the Church by the Port, and it has nothing to do with *llong* meaning ship. The case for the poem in the Black Book of Carmarthen belonging to the Battle of Llongborth at Langport, Somerset, and Geraint being identified with the Geruntius of Dumnonia is considered to be well-established by scholars, although I have to say that I have my reservations. Everyone calls this poem the Geruntius poem, which in itself conditions one to assume that it is what they say it is.

Clearly there was a Geraint of some note in the early history of this part of Cardiganshire in West Wales, and this is the one that may have been contemporary with Arthur. The poem in the Black Book says *Geraint fil Erbin* meaning *ab Erbin* or son of Erbin. Now in several Welsh romances incorrectly but often called 'Mabinogion' such as *Culhwch and Olwen,* and the *Dream of Rhonabwy,* there is a *Geraint mab Erbin,* Geraint's son Erbin.' The same name occurs in one of the Welsh Triads where he figures as one of the seafarers of *Ynys Prydain* or the land of the South Britons. This Geraint therefore who is the father of Erbin could belong to an earlier period, and possibly be the contemporary of Arthur. In the absence of a Llongborth near Tresaith we have to say we do not know what battle occurred near there, and no one knows who was fighting whom. It could have resulted in the Geraint of *Din Gereint* of Cardigan losing his castle, for his apparent grave is some miles inland from Tresaith; it is even further from Cardigan where he would have been expected to be buried if he had not lost the battle. There is another story, Geraint and Enid which is derived from a French story called *Erec et Enide* by Chrétien de Troyes; this is a piece of French romantic fiction that may have been based on the Cardiganshire Geraint, but the writer of the Welsh version as *Geraint and Enid* has confused things by mixing what he knew of the Geruntius poem with the French Arthurian romance that he 'translated.'

At the present time we must leave it at that; unless a better case can be put forward identifying the poem of the *Battle of Llongborth* with the Cardiganshire site and the Age of Arthur. The present state of knowledge is unsatisfactory because of the uncertainties concerning two Geraints, one of whom is the father of Erbin and the other of whom is the son of Erbin; with the identification of Llongborth; and with the anachronistic mention of Arthur at the battle, assuming it was the one at Langport.

6. THE BATTLE OF CAMLAN

The battle of Camlann which Crawford said sometimes comes down to us in the garbled form of Camelon, I do not believe could have been in Cornwall, and this site is only based on Geoffrey from an interpolation in the *Brut.* Crawford supported a site on Hadrian's Wall called Camboglanna (Birdoswald) and in this he is supported by Jackson, but this case seems to rest on Camboglanna being a Latinization of Camblan; it is retained in its Welsh form of Camlann in the Latin text of the Harleian manuscript of the *Historia Brittonum.* An alternative proposed by Skene was the old roman fort at Camelon which would probably still have been usable by Arthur and his warrior-band at that time. Across the river from Camelon there was the singular building called Arthur's O'n or oven, and I shall treat of this in a separate chapter. But all of this assumes that Arthur was still in the North years later, when that battle took place. There is a wealth of tradition relating to this battle in the Welsh Triads and the *Vera Historia de Morte Arthuri,* and whilst the material in the former includes some items of northern origin, the latter takes up the story after the battle when Arthur receives an additional wound from a spear (a weapon favoured by the warriors of Gwynedd) and asks to be taken to Guenedote (Gwynedd), implying that the battle was in Wales. To accept a northern location for this battle one would have to believe that the traditions concening it in the Triads are all of northern origin, and that the *Vera Historia* is a fake; it follows on from where Geoffrey and the *Brut* leave off, but it contains totally different material of apparently Welsh origin.

I have already said that there is a tradition implying that after fighting the 'Saxons,' Arthur spent most of his life in what is now North Wales. There is a wealth of geographical place-name data to support this, as well as references in the Welsh literature and poems such as the Triads. The *Welsh Classical Dictionary* tells us that *Cam + llan* = crooked enclosure or *cam + glan* = crooked bank and that one possible site is marked on the O.S. map as *Cwm y llan,* or *Cwmllan* on the south side of Snowdon. In his *Celtic Folklore* John Rhys writes: "Arthur and his following set out from Dinas Emrys and crossed Hafod y Borth Mountain for a place above the upper reach of Cwmllan, called Tregalan, where they found their antagonists. From Tregalan the latter were pushed up the bwlch or pass, towards Cwm Dyli; but when the vanguard of the army with Arthur leading had reached the top of the pass, the enemy discharged a shower of arrows at them. There Arthur fell, and his body was buried in the pass so that no enemy might march that way so long as Arthur's dust rested there." John Rhys traced this story back only to an article in the *Brython* in 1861. There are problems with it because Gerald of Wales said that in North Wales they fought with spears, and only in South Wales with bows and arrows, but the pass mentioned above translates as 'the Pass of the Arrows.' There is also a sequel to this legend saying that a farmer seeking a lost sheep accidentally found the cave in which Arthur's warriors were sleeping "in countless numbers resting on their armour." This all sounds as though it has been based on late tradition, and here Arthur's knights are sleeping, presumably on twelfth-century armour; but he is dead! Perhaps the Cwmllan site was spotted by some nineteenth century gentleman who wanted to have an article published and found a suitable legend. Cwmllan in

Welsh means the church in the valley, a common enough name but it is not Camlan; only the legend there could have any meaning, but it has not been traced back before the nineteenth century. It may well be based on older material; also the second one about the cave, but the only likely history here is in the sequel which supports the idea that Arthur lies in a cave.

Also in Wales there is an Afon Gamlan or River Camlan near Dolgellau, and the name Camlan can be found more than once on the map near Dinas Mawddwy to the east of Dolgellau in North Wales. There is a hillside just north of Dinas Mawddwy called Camlan; it is on the road that goes west over the high mountain pass to Dolgellau. It is little more than a kilometre from that pass and it or the pass could be a place for a battle.

But the name of Camlan is also well-preserved just south of Dinas Mawddwy. On the west side of the River Dovey between Dinas Mawddwy and Mallwyd there are three farms named *Camlan-isaf* or Lower Camlan, *Camlan-uchaf* or Upper Camlan, and *Maes-y-camlan* or the Field of Camlan. The hillside above these farms is called Camlan, and on its slopes there is another farm called *Bron-camlan* or Breast of Camlan. The cover photo of this book shows the slopes of Camlan and the plain of the Dovey between *Maes-y-camlan* and *Camlan-uchaf.* If nothing else, these sites underline the likelihood that it is somewhere in this region that the Battle of Camlan was fought. Whilst this does not prove the site of the Battle of Camlan conclusively, it does have the merit of being the only place bearing that name several times over. Other proposed sites such as Camboglanna require one to believe that Arthur ended up in the North. The Welsh location

99

accords with the tradition that Arthur spent much of his later life in North Wales. The battle of Camlan is not given in Nennius, though it is in the Welsh Annals appended thereto. The reason it is not mentioned in Nennius may be because whoever put together what we call Nennius or the *Historia Brittonum* had a list of Arthur's battles in a campaign against the 'Saxons,' and that Camlan did not belong to that list because it was fought between two Cymric or Welsh-speaking groups.

The Camlan sites near Dinas Mawddwy are clearly marked on the Ordinance Survey map, and this just goes to show how much time the writers of Arthurian books have spent looking at the map of Wales. I support a site in Wales as most probable for this battle. The site on or below the pass north of Dinas Mawddwy is a candidate for a battle where one war-band is defending the route over the pass against an invading one; the site south by the plain of the Dovey would suit more a pre-arranged pitched battle of the 'we'll meet you at dawn and settle this once and for all' type. A battle-site on a plain also fits the fact that slopes and steep hillsides were often impenetrably wooded, inter-sected only by diagonal leys or narrow tracks used for driving domestic stock up to the high pastures in summer. Each of the named Camlan sites are plausible, but the second idea of a pre-arranged contest could suit the end of a long-standing feud when the boil was about to burst. Amongst the alleged survivors of the Battle of Camlan are Morgan ap Tegid who is associated with the region of Lake Bala in North Wales, St. Pedrog who has associ-ations with Cornwall but is said to originate from Wales, and St. Cynwyl about whom little is known but who seems to be linked with Wales, possibly the region of Lake Bala.

It has generally been assumed, following Geoffrey and the *Brut*, that Arthur was fighting Medrawd who had rebelled (and some say his force consisted of Picts, Scots and Saxons, though this is not convincing); but in the Welsh Annals we read only 'the Battle of Camlan in which Arthur and Medrawd fell.' It does not say who was fighting whom, but in the Welsh Triads we find that two of the unrestrained ravagings of the Island of Britain relate to Arthur and Medrawd. The first was when Medrawd came to Arthur's court and dragged Gwenhywfar from her chair and struck her. The second was when Arthur came to Medrawd's court and left neither food nor drink there. The Triads also say that Camlan was the worst of the futile battles of Britain and that it was caused by Gwenhwyfach striking a blow upon Gwenhywfar who was her older sister. Gwenhwyfach seems to have been Medrawd's wife. Another Triad names Gwenhywfar as the most unfaithful of the wives of the Island of Britain because of the man that she shamed. In all this we can see evidence of a long-standing feud between Arthur and Medrawd, despite the Triads describing the latter as a Royal Knight that had beauty and wisdom in peace, whilst in war no one could stand up to him. There is also a story that Iddog Cord Prydain added fuel to the fire by telling Medrawd of Arthur's insults to him, when he could have kept his mouth shut in the interests of peace.

Civil wars and feuds, especially when they involve former friends, family or lovers are always more bitter than international or intertribal wars and disputes, because the emotions linking friends, family and lovers turn into the most passionate hatreds. I think the hints at a long-standing feud between Arthur and Medrawd fit the bill better than Geoffrey's claim that it was a rebellion, and that evidence for this battle being fought in mid-Wales rules out any possibility of it being fought against Picts, Scots and Saxons.

The account of Camlan in the *Brut* says that Arthur was taken to Avallach to have his wounds taken care of; then it ends abruptly with the words "and that is all that is said here of Arthur's death." I have already said that the *Vera Historia De Morte Arthuri* continues this story from more or less where the *Brut* leaves off. In it Arthur asks to be taken to Avallach in Gwynnedd and this supports the location of the Battle of Camlan on or near the plain of the Dovey near Mallwyd, for it is in Powys and not Gwynedd. (It also clearly implies that Avallach or Avalon is in Wales and not in Somerset; and there is worse still for Somerset; Arthur's exhumation at Glastonbury has been exposed as a fraud aimed at bolstering the tourist trade of the Abbey — see the book by Ray Gibbs.)

The battle of Camlan marked the end of the Arthurian era. The Battle of Chester, around 613 A.D. isolated the North Britons from those in the South. Already isolated from the people of Dumnonia (Devon-Cornwall), the South Britons developed the idea of Wales and the Welsh nation and kept their independence, Norman intrusions apart, until the time of Edward I, when Llywellyn ap Gruffudd was killed. In the North the battle of Arfderydd in 573, near the Solway Firth, marked the victory of Rhydderch over an army of pagan and apostate British, and the establishment of the kingdom of Strathclyde-Cumbria with its seat on the natural fortress of *Alclyde* on Dumbarton Rock that lasted until 890 A.D., or thereabouts.

7. ARTHUR'S OVEN

I have given this item separate treatment because it will be referred to several times in succeeding chapters. Across the river Carron from Camelon in Stirlingshire, about three kilometres north of Falkirk, there stood an undoubtedly Roman building of singular appearance, being circular and with a domed roof. The dome was constructed by corbelling, followed by cutting away the projecting parts and smoothing off the curvature on both the outside and inside. It was so well constructed of polished ashlars that some who saw it said it was difficult to make out the joints between the stones. There was a door on the east, and the flat circular stone floor within had a diameter of about nineteen feet six inches. Above the door there was a sub-rectangular window. The central part of the roof seemed to have fallen in when descriptions were made in the eighteenth century, but it was probably completely domed over, otherwise the window above the door would have been unnecessary. In 1743 this building was demolished by the landowner and all the stones, even the foundation ones, were carted away and used to repair a mill-dam; it was the architectural scandal of that century.

Exterior of Arthur's O'n, after Stukeley's Carausius of 1757.

Some drawings of this building had been made from direct observation prior to its demolition and others had been made based on an architectural survey. To begin with, we have illustrations published by William Stukeley in 1757, above and 1720, below.

Section of Arthur's O'n after Stukeley's pamphlet of 1720.

Gordon's drawing of exterior of Arthur's O'n, 1726

Stukeley had not visited the site, however, and his drawings were based on a survey made by an architect named Andrew Jelfe. They are therefore like a tentative reconstruction of the building without much reference to its condition. However we also have drawings made by Gordon in 1726 that show the somewhat dilapidated state of it at that time.

This leaves us asking ourselves what it looked like when it was first built. Well, Gordon was criticized as lacking in thoroughness in his work, and Stukeley for having worked from second-hand information, but we have the recently discovered drawings of John Adair, printed in the article by Brown and Vasey. They are not reproduced here for they confirm that Stukeley and Gordon had the basic shape correct, but they seem to emphasize the smoothness of the close-fitting polished masonry. It is possible that Stukeley had seen Adair's drawings before he did the drawing for *Carausius* published in 1757. Many suggestions have been made as to the purpose of this building but the most likely one is that it was a shrine or a monument. The most useful source of information concerning this structure is by Steer: *Arthur's O'n: A Lost Shrine of Roman Britain.*

In some of the manuscripts of Nennius we find added a statement implying that the Emperor Carausius built a round house of polished stone on the bank of the River Carron as a triumphal arch after he had reinforced the Antonine Wall. A glance at the drawings that have been made of the building shows that it fits more a shrine or monument than a triumphal arch, and this would indicate that Carausius built this 'round house' as a thanksgiving or commemoration of his construction work. It is certainly a very special building judging by the quality and smooth finish of the stonework that may imply legionary workmanship. The corbelled dome makes it unique for its time, and the only item that we can compare it with is on a fragment of Roman sculpture from Rose Hill, between Birdoswald and Carvoiran on Hadrian's Wall; it is illustrated in the article by Steer. The carving includes a winged victory flying, a legionary eagle with outstretched wings, and a domed building with a tree giving the impression of a shrine, possibly in a sacred grove. The similarity of this dome with the one of Carausius is striking, and it may well be a representation of it, completely domed over as it was when it was first built. Although the original name of our building appears to have been associated with that of Carausius, there are also links with that of Julius Caesar in the fifteenth and sixteenth centuries, and I add herebelow the account from John of Fordun's *Chronicle of the Scottish Nation*. After telling us that Julius Caesar was sent news that the Gauls had rebelled again, Fordun writes:

"Accordingly, apprehending that these matters were of more importance than the subjugation of those kings [of northern Britain] Caesar determined to sail across to Gaul, but being uncertain as to his return, he hastily caused a small round chamber, like a pigeon-house, and of no use, apparently, but as a landmark, to be built of large smooth stones, without mortar, not far from the mouth of the river Carron; and he wanted to build the little chamber as marking the extreme limit of the Roman possessions to the north-west, almost at the world's end, and as a lasting monument of his military renown; just as Hercules of old planted pillars in the island of Gades, at the western extremity of Europe, as a memorial of his eternal fame and long drawn labours. Another version, that especially of common report, is that Julius Caesar had this chamber carried about with him by the troops, with each stone separate and built up again from day to day, wherever they halted, that he might rest therein more safely than in a tent; but that, when he was in a hurry to return to Gaul, he left it behind with the intention of coming back without delay; and that it was built up with one stone merely laid upon one another, as is to be seen to this day. On the east side of the chamber, there is an entrance so large that an armed soldier on horseback can pass in without touching the top of the doorway with the crested helmet on his head. This Julius defeated the fierce nation of the Gauls in many battles, and finally, sailing over into Britain, extended the Roman Empire beyond the barrier of the ocean; all of which he accomplished within ten years."

The problem with the two versions of the story quoted by Fordun is that the first one seems unlikely because the type of construction does not indicate a building put up in a hurry. The second version, however, gets round this problem by saying that the polished and pre-shaped stones had been made long before the erection on the site near the Carron. One's credibility is, however, stretched to the limit in imagining that Caesar's troops had to take down and rebuild this edifice every time he moved on his campaigns. Fordun himself does not claim to support this version but merely tells us that it is of "common report." The simplest approach is to regard this as a building of Roman origin, possibly marking the limit of the Roman province, probably attributable to Carusius rather than to Caesar.

Steer tells us that the oldest written reference to this building as Arthur's O'n or oven, in Latin as *furnace Arthuri*, is in the charter of Newbattle Abbey dated 1293. There is, however, a very probable earlier reference to it in the *Liber Floridus* written by Lambert de St. Omer, the Latin text of which says that there is a palace in Pictland that belonged to Arthur the warrior in which his exploits and wars are sculptured. No doubt this relates to Arthur's O'n but the sculptures if they were present were probably Roman. Some of the people that examined the interior of Arthur's O'n before it was demolished thought they saw some evidence of sculpture, for example of an eagle with outstretched wings, but the various reports were vague and contradictory because they were made with inadequate lighting. Another report was of an obviously later addition, of St George within a shield. From the available literature this building appears to have been called Carausius' vault from the arched roof implied by the Latin *fornix*, Arthur's Palace, Arthur's O'n or oven from the Latin *fornax*, an oven or kiln; from Caesar, Julius's Hoff, meaning Hove; and finally Arthur's Hove; hoff or hove meaning hall. Furthermore the two Latin words *fornix* and *fornax* are equally descriptive of the structure, for it has an arched vaulted roof and it does look like an oven or kiln. Clearly this building was known first as associated with the Roman occupation, later with Arthur.

8. DID ARTHUR EXIST

In my life-time there have been books, papers, rumours or gossip claiming that umpteen famous characters never really existed. The list includes Socrates, Lao Zi or the Old Master of ancient China, Lie Zi another Chinese sage, Jesus, King Arthur, Shakespeare, Robin Hood, Homer, Agamemnon, Ulysses and so on. Many of these are persons whom people, including the young, could look up to for a higher ideal than that which is presented by ordinary life. I find the motives of some of these debunkers disturbing and see them as part of the process that is turning the masses into homogenized modernized morons who know nothing of life beyond what is presented to them in the soap operas and tabloids, the adoration of ordinary life and so-called celebrities, and who no longer have any ideals which they can look up to or live by. There is no organised conspiracy here; many of the modern debunkers have no doubt acted from a sincere belief that they were pursuing or presenting the truth about some character of alleged history, but in sum, and even if it were not their intention, they add up to a general trend to do away with the idealism that many of those personages represented.

Socrates differed from many of his literary and philosophical contemporaries in that he did not write books, so the main evidence we have of him is second-hand, in the dialogues written by Plato and Xenophon.

Lao Zi, the Old Master of Daoism wrote a most famous book called the *Dao de Jing (Tao-te-king)* that has been translated into almost as many languages as the Bible. Of him, the celebrated Chinese historian Sima Qian wrote around 100 B.C: '....of the Old Master we can only be sure that, having loved obscurity above all, he deliberately covered up the traces of his life.' Lie Zi never wrote, but in the book that bears his name it is said that when he was about to leave his province because of famine, his followers asked him to go over his teaching with them. No doubt they took notes that formed the skeleton of the book that we now know as the '*Chong Hu Chen Jing.*' A recent translation of a later Chinese work, *the Book of Chuang Tzu* (Zhuang Zi) by Martin Palmer implies that it is the oldest Book of Daoism because Lao Zi probably did not exist. He also states that the Book of Lie Zi only dates from 600 years after the time of that author; but I have already indicated the probable origin of that book from notes taken down by Lie Zi's contemporaries.

Jesus was only mentioned in passing by one contemporary writer, Josephus, in *The Jewish Wars.* All of the Christian writings date from after his time so that the historical 'evidence' for his having existed is slight. But Jesus didn't write a book, nor did he fight a battle, so it is not surprising that he left no contemporary mark on history and all that we know of him comes from accounts of his life and teaching that were not written down until later. The four Gospels have been altered less than the Acts of the Apostles, but no doubt they have undergone some editing with interpolations and deletions; yet in substance they still belong to their original authors.

Shakespeare left a tomb, but so little evidence of his life that there have been those that doubted if he ever existed or if his writings were not due to Francis Bacon writing under a synonym. Needless to say the majority are still pleased to believe in a historical Shakespeare.

Robin Hood and his Welsh counterpart Twm Shôn Catti have become so surrounded by fabulous adventures as to lead some to question if either of them ever really existed.

But we must be careful to separate the fabulous tales from the real person around whom they have been woven. In Beddgellert, Wales, there is the moving story of Prince Llewellyn who left his child in the care of his favourite dog Gellert. On his return Gellert ran up to greet him covered in blood. Thinking the dog had killed his child he drew his sword and killed it, only to discover moments later that it had protected it from a wolf that lay dead nearby. This is a sad tale that has moved many to tears, but we now know that it is based on a well-known central European legend. It seems that early in the nineteenth century the landlord of the local tavern asked the vicar how they could attract the new tourists to the place that is now called Beddgellert. The vicar came up with this legend and the landlord had a plaque erected with the tale written upon it, citing Prince Llewellyn as the main character. Prince Llewellyn is, of course, a genuine person from Welsh history, but this serves well to show how fabulous tales can so easily become attached to such people, even more so as their fame increases. The original version of this story, which obviously does not belong to Prince Llewellyn, may have been pure fiction, but there may be some historical character somewhere in European history that it belonged to.

The existence of Arthur has been questioned or denied a number of times, and I think the best way of dealing with this is to go through the argument against a historical Arthur point by point. The argument has been summed up in a well-written, scholarly paper entitled *The Nature of Arthur* by O. J. Padel (1994). I shall endeavour to report the argument against a probable historical Arthur as accurately as I can; followed by my own comments. I apologize if I fail to do this as well as some might expect.

The argument begins by saying that the accepted opinion of recent scholars is that Arthur may well have existed as a sixth-century leader of the combined British resistance against the Saxon invaders. It goes on to say that all the scholars have started by looking in the pre-Galfredian literature, that is literature from before the time of Geoffrey of Monmouth, for what they consider to be accounts of the historical Arthur and taken them separately from any mythological accounts of those times. It claims that if one takes the same literature and looks at it another way, taking the Arthurian mythology and landscape names of Scotland, Wales, Cornwall and Brittany, then one sees the possible historical evidence in a different perspective. This leads those who support this argument to say that looked at this way one can say that Arthur may have existed but he probably did not, rather than that he probably did. I should hardly need to remind readers that many of the persons listed at the beginning of this chapter left little or no contemporary mark on history.

Padel begins by stating that the *Historia Brittonum* includes the earliest Arthurian text we have, and that the evidence of Arthur in Welsh poetry of earlier date is problematical because these poems are notoriously impossible to date. He does not comment on Sir Ifor Williams conclusion that in the *Book of Taliesin* there were twelve poems likely to be of sixth-century origin. I have already pointed out that the philologist Toby Griffen, also writing in 1994, cautiously agreed with Ifor Williams, stating that some of the twelve poems could well be from the sixth century, others a little later. Griffen likewise concluded that the original text of the *Gododdin* dated from early in the seventh century, but that it has come to us as a copy of a copy of a copy...etc. In it there is a single reference to Arthur implying that he was a mighty hero:

"He fed black ravens on the rampart of a fortress
Though he was no Arthur."

The argument continues by stating that the apparent historical evidence of Arthur's battles in Nennius must be taken alongside the two mythological stories that are in the *memorabilia*, or Marvels of Britain, appended to Nennius, and which carry equal weight. The *memorabilia* were included in the manuscript of 820-30, but Richard Rowley thinks they were transcribed by 'Nennius' or pre-Nennius from a source different to the chronicles that precede them.

Much of the argument is based on the fact that in pre-Galfredian times the name of Arthur figured in the mythology, folk-lore and landscape features of Scotland, Wales, Cornwall and Brittany. But the history of those times, as I have already mentioned, tells us that many of the nobles of the northern Cymry lost their territories as a result of pressure from the devastations of the Picts and Scots. Some of the refugee dispossessed nobles often with their retinues would move down into Wales and Cornwall. Some of them founded monasteries, and even travelled as far as Brittany before finally settling. Add to this the advent of the yellow plague which came to the Christian parts of Britain and caused many to flee to Brittany, and we have a picture of influential people with

113

their culture and place names moving from the North into what are now Wales, Cornwall and Brittany. The beginnings of this migration were before Arthur's campaign, but there seems to have been a continuing migration to Brittany especially around the time of the yellow plague near the mid-sixth century. It is not surprising therefore that the stories of Arthur and the fables that developed around his name, often associated with local landscape features, can be found repeatedly from Scotland all the way to Brittany. This renaming of landscape features and development of fabulous tales no doubt also suited the new Christian monks who were looking for means of replacing pagan heroes and land-markers with names associated with the new religion. They did the same thing with the pagan holy wells, giving each one the name of a Christian saint and an appropriate legend! Later on it suited the interests of the Anglo-Norman kings and their new aristocracy who were anxious, through their ancient British ancestry, to claim that they had a right to rule where they were ruling. No doubt they encouraged the planting of legends and fabrication of place-names here and there following the publication of Geoffrey's *History*.

(For those who are not familiar with the story of the yellow plague, I add that it seems to have followed on the great eruption of Krakatoa when there were clouds of yellow sulphurous fumes drifting around, which coincided with an epidemic of bubonic plague; this came to the Christians in Britain and caused a considerable migration to Brittany which was under-populated at that time. The plague came through the old shipping routes from the Mediterranean; the pagan Saxons are said to have largely missed it because they were trading with the Baltic States and not the Mediterranean; Brittany was probably safer

114

because the population there was small and they were doing little overseas trading. Many place-names in Brittany are clearly imported from the regions of the South Britons.)

Three of the so-called Ancient Books of Wales, the *Book of Taliesin*, the *Gododdin* and the *Black Book of Carmarthen* seem to include material that originated in the North, and which was brought down south by refugee monks. The argument continues by saying that the existence of more than one Arthur's oven, etc., in different parts of Britain is evidence that there is no original or historical basis for any of them, but I think the history of population movements and the advent of Christianity help to explain much, although I must add the sheer amount of Arthurian names in landscape features, etc., is astonishing. Arthur must have become, as they say, a legend in his own time.

Apart from saying that there is more than one Arthur's Oven in Britain, Padel states that the one in Stirlingshire only became known as such in the thirteenth century, but that it was of Roman origin. Surely the thirteenth century is simply the time when it first surfaced to appear in English literature and it had probably been known by that name to local people long before. Another scholar, David Dumville suggested that Arthur was possibly deliberately substituted for Carutius or that scribal corruption caused the replacement, and that the similarity between *fornix*, a vault and *fornax* an oven was suspicious. It seems likely that Dumville had never bothered to see the various drawings of Arthur's O'n, and he admits in a footnote to one of his papers that it was Kenneth Jackson who told him that the building did in fact look like an oven. I have already pointed out that there is no need to contrive a derivation of the name Arthur's O'n from Carutius' vault, for the function of this building may have changed from that of a Roman shrine or monument to another usage when it became associated with the name of Arthur, and *fornix* and *fornax* are equally descriptive alternatives for this building: the ceiling inside is vaulted and when new it almost certainly formed a complete dome, hence Carutius' vault from its original purpose; later, when the middle part of the roof had fallen in, it looked like a kiln or oven, hence Arthur's Oven, from a later usage. Personally I do not see this beehive-shaped Roman building with its flat circular floor in any way as evidence against a historical Arthur. Padel also states that 'recent enthusiasts' have wished to locate Arthur in Scotland and that there is no reason to give this priority. My own view is that Arthur came from what is now Wales but spent enough time in the North to leave an imprint there before spending much of the rest of his life in North Wales. I have already pointed out that W. F. Skene and Stuart Glennie put forward serious arguments back in the eighteen sixties for Scotland as a historic home of Arthuriana; also Loth in 1934; and they are hardly 'recent enthusiasts.' Skene was a pioneer, but he was also a scholar, despite which he tends to be ignored these days. A. O. Anderson the respected historian and compiler of the *Early Sources of Scottish History* commented that although it has become fashionable to scoff at Skene, in fact much of his work 'still stands.'

Another claim made is that the four British leaders in the next generation called Arthur were all Irish settlers, and that with the possible exception of Brittany, the British were avoiding using the name because of their awe of Arthur as a god-like mythological character. Griffen, on the other hand sees the existence of four British military

116

leaders of the same name in the generation after Arthur as evidence that Arthur really did exist in history, and that they were named thus because of his prowess. Griffen points out that before the sixth century there was no evidence for Arthur as a name, whereas after the time of Arthur it became popular.

Padel goes on to say, quite rightly, that in the oldest extant but fire-damaged manuscript of Gildas there are no paragraph divisions, and the account of the Battle of Badon therefore follows on the account of Ambrosius Aurelianus as a successful leader of the Britons. This could be taken as implying that the Battle of Badon was won by Ambrosius and not by Arthur. However, one must note that whoever first copied the text of Gildas into paragraphs must have considered the Badon item as separate from the preceding material. In any case Gildas would have been more likely to ascribe a victory to a ruler than a military commander, and I do not see in this any reason for denying the historicity of Arthur whom Malmesbury, rightly or wrongly, said was the helper of Ambrosius.

Padel goes on to imply that Arthur probably never existed outside of fable and that his appearance as a British leader fighting the Saxons had been deliberately 'historicized'. He claims that the legendary Arthur is the primary one and that by the time of the *Historia Brittonum* he had started to attract pseudo-historical material to his name.

In support of the foregoing he points out the close parallel between Arthur and Fionn in Ireland who also featured in legends connected with the landscape and whose band of young warriors were almost independent

117

of society and with a rôle as defenders of Ireland, even anachronistically against the Scandinavians, just as Arthur is depicted as defending Britain from the Saxon invaders. Like Arthur, there is a legend that Fionn and his warriors would return one day, but some think this was borrowed from the Arthurian legend. The Annals of Tigernac contain an entry for Fionn's death under the year 283, and Padel claims that this 'historicized' entry has been attributed to the eleventh century. I would add, however that one cannot categorically say that there was not a historical personage behind the legendary Fingal or Fionn, no more than one can categorically deny it. Padel concludes that there is no reason for supposing there was ever a historical Fionn, and that the wealth of Arthurian legend and folklore that existed before the time of Geoffrey of Monmouth represents the real Arthur, and that the historical character was a literary accretion. The only slender 'evidence' left, he says, is that most of the legends of persons that are sleeping to come again refer to actual historical personages such as Charlemagne, Owain Glendŵr and so on. One of the problems with this parallel between Fionn and Arthur and their war-bands being used to deny the historicity of Arthur, is that one can draw exactly the same parallel between Arthur and Charlemagne, whom Padel admits as a person in history. I quote here from the book by Charles Hardwick:

"Karl de Gross, a German by birth, name and language was a warrior who conquered nearly the whole of Europe and founded one of the most important dynastic houses of mediaeval times. He was born about the year 742 in the castle of Silzberg, in Bavaria, and died in 814 at Aachen, now called Aix-la-Chapelle. This person is a character of history. On the other hand the Charlemagne of romance is a mythical personage. He is supposed to be a Frenchman at a time when neither the French nation nor the French language can properly be said to have existed; and he is represented as a doughty crusader, although crusading was not thought of until after the Carolingian era. He is a myth. If in his case legend were not controlled by history, he would be for us as unreal as Agamemnon... To the historic Karl corresponds in many particulars the mythical Charlemagne. The legend has preserved the fact, which without the information supplied by history we might perhaps set down as a fiction, that there was a time when Germany, Gaul, Italy, and part of Spain formed a single empire. And as Mr Freeman has well observed: 'the mythical crusades of Charlemagne are good evidence that there *were* crusades, although the real Karl had nothing whatever to do with one.'" Here we have a parallel between Charlemagne and his knights with Arthur and his warrior-knights, but where the former is accepted as a character of history.

Furthermore, Padel's claim that there is no reason for supposing a historical Fionn can be questioned. There is certainly no written historical evidence, but if one takes the no smoke without fire view one can at least wonder if there were not some historical basis. Glennie stressed the remarkable parallel between Arthurian tales and topography and Fennian or Fingalian ones, without seeing in that any reason for doubting the existence of a historical Arthur, and I take the same point of view. What we are dealing with there is a warrior tradition common to Picts, Scots and Britons in which, just as today young people go travelling before becoming trapped in a career, so young men would attach themselves to a warrior-leader with whom they could seek adventure and experience for a

119

time; and possibly also spiritual guidance. Anyone that has read the famous episode in the Indian Mahabarata known as the Gita, which deals with karma yoga or a way of action, will realise that even the warrior class in ancient times had a spiritual way, and I shall comment on this further in the next chapter. The same holds good also for the native originals of many of the varieties of oriental martial arts that have been imported into the West; they often had a spiritual basis or objective behind their psycho-physical side, but which has generally been lost in their Western presentations.

As regards the allegations of historicizing by interpolating dates in old chronicles, the very use of that word is influencing the reader, and one does not know whether a date has been added for that purpose or by someone acting from a belief that they were editing and updating a chronicle with a genuine date taken from another source. I see Scotland as the home of a part but not all of the Arthurian Saga, and the wealth of local legend relating to Arthurian characters there as evidence of a possible historical basis behind the mediaeval fictions. The other and main part of the Arthurian Saga belongs to Wales, but we must remember that in the sixth century neither Wales nor Scotland existed such as we know them today.

Many of those who argue against a historical Arthur deny the approach that there is no smoke without fire. One should be careful, however, in knocking this idea. To quote a single example, Ray Gibbs tells us that in the nineteenth century in the pub at Wedmore in Somerset they used to tell a yarn about sailing ships coming across the moors and tying up outside. Everyone smiled at this silly tale, but early in the twentieth century the vicar, a Mr.

Hervey, organized a dig in the little stream outside the pub and six feet down they found shards of red Samian ware of Italian origin, indicating that there had been a navigable waterway there in Roman times and that trading vessels would come bringing wine, pottery and other produce from the Mediterranean and leave with silver-lead from the Mendips. No doubt the reader will have come across other examples of this type from time to time, and for this reason one should be careful about rejecting what one reads in the *Brut*, for example, for behind the embellishments one can find some history.

One useful thing that Padel brought up is that the best possible candidate for a historical Arthur invading Gaul and taking on the Roman Empire would be one Lucius Artorius Castus, a Roman centurion who was sent to Brittany to lead two legions against the Armoricans. Geoffrey Ashe has named a Riothamus as an alternative candidate for this episode, but Griffen does not support this, and adds that there has been muddling because earlier, Maximus had invaded Europe from Britain and his exploits were fairly similar to those of Riothamus, and Maximus appears in the Mabinogion collection in the *Dream of Macsen Wledig*. Griffen adds that both Maximus and Riothamus could have been *sources* for the continental episode in the *Brut* and Geoffrey, but they were never Arthur. Whatever the truth, almost everyone believes that the European campaign ascribed to Arthur by the *Brut* and Geoffrey has nothing to do with any British Arthur.

Much of Padel's argument appears to be convincing at the time of reading, but on reflection I find that if I turn to Griffen's book where much of the same 'evidence' is treated from the point of view of philological detective work, I still find the case for a historical Arthur impressive. Griffen concludes with "the fact is that our Arthur — and Aneirin's Arthur, and the Welsh Annals' Arthur — lived in the early sixth century, was a great military leader, and gave rise to legends of his own before his legends were combined with those of Riothamus, Maximus, and others."

At the end of the day I have to say that it is impossible to prove or disprove the existence of a historical Arthur; the volume of legendary material compared with the few possible historical references is impressive, but if the historical Arthur were also a spiritual leader he may well have left but few traces of his life as has happened with many other characters, some of whom I mentioned at the beginning of this chapter. Most people will choose what they want to believe, or simply sit on the fence. I am still strongly inclined to believe in a historical Arthur, although I must add that the symbolism in tales such as *Sir Gawain and the Green Knight* and the *Quest of the Grail* still holds good in either case, and is therefore not affected by any affirmation or denial. Finally I must add that the article by Padel came out in 1994, six years before the publication of the works by Blake and Lloyd, and that their investigation of Arthurian localities in Wales and their probable relationships to Welsh Arthurian literature adds strength to the case for a historical Arthur.

9. ARTHUR GURU AND THE QUEST

For want of anything more appropriate, I have used the now familiar Sanskrit word guru here, though it has been abused and debased in modern times. It implies a spiritual master, providing one takes the word master in its older sense of teacher and guide; a true spiritual master is never a power seeker as are so many of the fakes of modern times. It is perhaps for this reason that the historical Arthur, like Socrates, Jesus, Lao-tzu and others of a profound and spiritual nature, has left little trace of his own life. One thing that emerges from some aspects of what one might term the traditional and legendary material is that Arthur does not appear so much as a land-grabber seeking a territory to rule over as were the founders of most dynasties, but as a person presiding over a group of young warriors as their mentor or guide as well as their military leader.

I have included the Arthurian text of the *Brut* in this book; it already contains the Merlin of mythology who has no clear historical basis but who may have been Arthur's Druid advisor. The Merlin of mythology certainly does not figure in early Welsh poetry, but I remind readers that Peter Roberts commented that "Arthur is said to have been rebuked by a hermit for his attachment to diviners." It was the publication of Geoffrey's Latin text, which he presented to the world as 'history,' that prompted the appearance of umpteen Arthurian romances, all based on Arthur as King or even Emperor with his knights in the panoply of the twelfth century, and their ladies. I do not intend to revue that literature here; there are Arthurian encyclopaedias and the like in which the reader can find the references. What I do intend to consider is the inclusion in that literature of stories of the spiritual ideal such as *Sir Gawain and the Green Knight* and the *Quest of* the *Grail*, and possible precursors such as the ancient poem from the Book of Taliesin commonly called the *Spoils of Annwn* and a pre-Galfredian Welsh romance called *Peredur.*

At this point I must digress for I find now, after some two centuries of materialistic secular education, that very few people have any notion of what is meant by spiritual development and transformation. Ordinary or exoteric religion provides people with a set of rules to live by and a ritual to participate in that is aimed at ensuring that they will not suffer after death, and most people can easily understand this, even if they do not believe it. Esoteric or hidden spirituality, on the other hand, aims to enable the adept to transform his or her being even during this life, and this was the secret of the saints and sages.

It will be impossible for me to treat the subject in full, but here are a few explanatory comments intended to show that the spiritual 'journey' leads to increased degrees of freedom and understanding; to a real and permanent change of being. In a sense this is lost knowledge; something that was common during the Age of the Saints of the early Celtic church in the sixth century, but which has become forgotten with the passage of time, for all human institutions including religions are subject to the cyclic laws of birth — growth — maturity — senility, until there comes a renewal of the cycle. Another writer might explain the same topic differently; all I am trying to do is introduce readers to some ideas compressed into a few paragraphs:

Sinbad the Sailor was shipwrecked seven times, corresponding with the seven heavens. The first time his ship sank, he consigned himself to the will of God and found himself washed up on the beach of an island. Just as he set out to climb up the steep rocky slope to the plateau above, a wizened little character, the Old Man of the Sea, cried out to him asking for a piggy back up to the top. Sinbad let him climb up on his shoulders but when they were at the top he locked his ankles round Sinbad's neck and gripped his ears firmly saying go here, go there, do this, do that, stand up, sit down, incessantly nagging him and pushing him around. Sinbad could not shake him off, but he had recourse to a stratagem. He got some rotten fruit and fermented it into a strong drink and let the old man partake of it until he was so drunk that he could shake him off onto the ground. Then he took a huge rock and smashed the old man to bits saying 'may God have no mercy on him,' for the old man is pure illusion; nothing more than ordinary people's collective desires that push them around all their lives. This destruction of the old man is the mysterious death and rebirth on this first part of the spiritual 'journey,' and the person from then on is twice-born, returned to the original state of true man or woman; and those who are truly twice-born are thereby free from the nagging desires that push ordinary folk around. This state can only be achieved through the appropriate spiritual practices and the grace or mercy of God. All their senses are heightened and the achievement of this state is accompanied by a feeling of freedom and wonder, and much more that one cannot easily put into words. I hardly need add that the modern 'twice-born' fundamentalists have given themselves this title without having the thing in question. Few indeed have achieved this state in modern times.

When ancient ideas seemed in danger of being lost, the knowledge of them was often hidden in places where it would persist unnoticed. The game of snakes and ladders, for example, would seem to be a way of hiding and preserving the notion of karma and rebirth; a ladder denoting good karma and a snake bad karma. It first seems to have appeared in India in the twelfth century and became popular in the West in the nineteenth. Hidden in the army we find another clue to the symbolism just mentioned in the tale of Sinbad the Sailor. In the regimental hierarchy of the army we have the ranks of colonel, captain, corporal, and private soldier. Now the word colonel corresponds on the one hand with the Italian *colonello*, a column representing the *axis mundi* or link between heaven and earth; and on the other hand, from its pronunciation, with the English kernel representing the centre of the fruit; in old French it was written *coronel* or *coronnel*. Similarly, in English the centre of the house is the hearth, which corresponds with the heart, and in French the centre of the old homesteads, especially in the south, was the *cour* or courtyard corresponding with the *coeur* or heart (cf. the kernal of the fruit and the old French *corronel*.) Now the heart in question here is not the pumping organ in the chest, but what it symbolises, the spiritual and intellectual centre of the being. This is the 'heart' of profound literature and poetry, the notion of which has been debased and sentimentalised in modern song and speech. The captain, from the cap on the head, represents the mind or mental faculty. The corporal represents the corpus or body, and the private the private parts. Thus we have a natural hierarchy in which the spirit controls the mind which in turn controls the bodily and sexual appetites. This sequence spirit-mind-body-sex is the normal state of 'twice-born' people, but ordinary people do not have this hierarchy intact so that they are often governed not by reason, but by their passions; and those in which that hierarchy is completely inverted are pushed around by their sex urges above all else. Readers should note that sex comes at the bottom of this hierarchy not because it is 'evil' in itself but because as the strongest biological urge, it needs the greatest amount of control. So the first part of the spiritual journey, represented by Sinbad the Sailor's ridding himself of the Old Man of the Sea, brings about the restoration of this hierarchy from whatever disordered state it was in before. After that, Sinbad can be called twice-born, from the death of the Old Man, and a True Man. This is the accomplishment of the first part of the spiritual journey, which brings about a freedom from the passions and desires that have been pushing one about.

This state of the twice-born, of primordial or true man (or woman) marks the restoration of the original human condition; but it is not the final end; it marks the beginning of the spiritual quest proper. There are seven heavens, and Sinbad the Sailor was shipwrecked seven times, each time achieving a superior state of being than the previous one. The ancient Greeks described the state of True Man as the accomplishment of the 'lesser mysteries' and the states beyond as belonging to the 'greater mysteries.' The notion of the seven heavens (of the greater mysteries) was hidden of all places in the famous dance of the seven veils in which each successive state is more alluring than the previous one, until finally the naked truth is revealed in all its glory!

To understand some of the methods or spiritual practices involved in this return to the true human state, we must first look at Indian cosmology where we find four ages in the present human cycle, which correspond with the old Western notions of an Age of Gold followed by one of Silver, Bronze, and finally Iron. The Age of Iron roughly corresponds with the historical period; in India it is called The Age of Kali, an age of darkness, warfare and troubles. Indian cosmology says that in the first Age people achieved the superior states of being by their spirit alone; later it was by sacrifice, but in this present Age of Kali it can be achieved through the practice of *mantra*, the repetition of a sacred name or phrase. This endless repetition of one and the same thing seems idiotic to those who do not understand it. Everything in the universe is rhythmic and repetitive, the movements of the planets, the regular course of the seasons, the tides of the oceans, the waves of the sea, the beating of the heart, the breathing cycle, and so on. Thus *mantra* (Sanskrit), *dhikr* (Arabic) or its Christian equivalent of the prayer of the heart puts one in harmony with the great rhythms of the universe, and that is why it 'works.' Now if we look into Christianity in the early days when saints or holy persons were abundant, we find very little reference to their methods which seem to have been personal and kept secret, but Paul Johnson tells us that St. Jerome repeated a phrase from one of the Psalms. We may conjecture that this sort of thing was common amongst the early Christians. In the Roman Church all that survived of this practice seems to be the rosary, the *Ave Maria*, but in the Orthodox Church which separated from the Roman one in 1050, we find a well-developed culture of repetitive prayer called the prayer of the heart, made famous by a little anonymous book called

The Way of a Pilgrim. There is also an Orthodox book entitled the *Philokalia* which supports the same practice.

I have already mentioned the symbolism of the heart as spiritual centre of the being. Achieving the state of the twice-born, of true man or woman corresponds in heart symbolism with knowing the outside of the heart. For example there is an Andalusian song which goes *tengo tu nombre apuntao en las murailles de mi corazon* — I have thy name written down on the walls of my heart. This is a *double-entendre* song which can be taken superficially as a love song, and more profoundly as referring to a survival of a Sufi practice of *dhikr* during the period of the Inquisition and beyond. As I have just said, *dhikr* is the Arabic word for mantra or the prayer of the heart and the Sufis say that the first spiritual 'station' corresponds with the prayer repeating itself on the outside of the heart. I shall return to this important point when we look at the meaning of the quest of the grail.

If we now return to Indian cosmology and literature, we find that in the practice of *yoga,* which implies travelling towards union with God, there are three basic spiritual ways, of love, knowledge and action. Those in a knightly or warrior class follow *karma-yoga* or a way of action, and the way in which they go about their active life is intimately linked with any spiritual progress they may make. I add this comment because we do not know to what extent, if any, a repetitive and rhythmic prayer of the heart or similar figured in the spiritual life of the knights of old. It is very probable that it did. I can only suggest that any readers that have not read the famous *Bhagavad Gita* from the Indian epic called the *Mahabarata* should do so if they find this topic interesting; this does not speak directly of

129

mantra but of the attitudes to be taken in the active life of a warrior. The battle of the *Mahabarata*, which Bond puts at February 18th 3102 B.C., marked the beginning in India of this present Age of Kali (cf. the western Age of Iron) for which mantra is recommended.

The passage into this present Age involved a change. In the previous Age people followed a way of sacrifice, whereas in the present one invocation (*mantra, dhikr* or the prayer of the heart) is the recommended practice. The passage from the previous age of sacrifice into the present one is marked in the Semitic tradition by Abraham who was reluctantly about to sacrifice his own son, when he was told that it was no longer necessary. Many readers these days should be sufficiently familiar with the martial arts that have been imported from China and Japan to know that they have or had a spiritual aspect to them, and that in some cases they use or used some form of mantra. Even as recent as the nineteenth century many of the warrior tribes that occupied the Great Plains of North America had secret societies in which they went beyond the ordinary observances of the rest of their tribe. Some moderns suffering from the sentimentalism that goes with modern materialism may be shocked to find profound spiritual practices among the warrior class, but I add that saints and sages attain their spiritual station not because of their faults, for example fighting in the warrior class, but despite them. I add that, unlike the pictures on Victorian stained-glass windows, the disciples of Jesus were armed, as is witnessed by one of them lopping off an ear with his sword at the time of Jesus's arrest. In Wales we find that each early monastery had a *Castell Mynach* or monk's Castle nearby where they could better defend themselves in case of attack. Up to the eighth century in Ireland the monasteries were expected to provide soldiers if the ruler of their territory went to war. In the symbolism of warfare we can see that the great holy war is the one fought against the evil within oneself, and not externally. We find in many of the tales of Arthur that he sends his knights out on quests of adventure but he does not take part in them himself, and this implies he had already achieved the quest within himself. Spiritual transformation such as I have described above is a very rare thing indeed in modern times, but one cannot understand the ancient world without knowing something about it; also when societies degenerate to rock-bottom there is sometimes a renewal that happens about as predictably as do changes in the weather; one never knows when or how. For a more detailed account of the esoteric way, see my book *The Way and the Quest.*

Now we can continue. Before going on to discuss specific items, we must consider their possible origins, and I begin this with a hypothetical scenario: Arthur was not just a war leader, but the spiritual teacher or master of an order of warriors or knights in the fifth/sixth century. Some support for part of this conjecture is given by Albert le Grand of Brittany who says that Hoel (Howel) the First founded an order of knights called 'L'ordre de l'Ermine,' and whilst this proves nothing, it could imply that spiritual orders of warrior knights were a feature of the ancient world, just as I have mentioned that they were amongst the Plains Indians even towards modern times. As in many esoteric bodies, that is groups that practised an inner spiritual life beyond just the rites and morality of exterior religion, secrecy was important, for the common people would not understand them. In many such organisations the assembled members would sit on the ground

131

in a circle the centre of which would temporarily be the centre of the world from which the *axis mundi* or spiritual 'pole' would ascend. This pattern is to be seen in the Christian Celtic wheel-crosses where the symbolism is centripetal, contrasted with the axial symbolism of the Latin cross. I suggest that Arthur's round table was nothing more than that; any flat circular floor where the knights or initiates of the Order of the Round Table sat for the performance of their rites. Even today, many Sufi groups sit thus for their meetings. In support of this I point out that the oldest reference to a 'round table' is by Wace who wrote in garbled French: *'fist Artus la reonde table.'* Now in French the adjective normally follows the noun. Therefore the noun is *reonde* meaning a rotunda, and *table* is the adjective implying tabulated. So we have Arthur made a tabulated rotunda, taking *fist* to be from *fit* meaning 'made' in the past historic tense. The word for table in Welsh is *bordd,* and in those days the food was served on a board on the floor and not a table with legs.

Now Arthur's campaign before he settled in North Wales seems to have taken him to the North that we now call Southern Scotland. I have already suggested that he may have spent some time at Camelon in Stirlingshire. There was formerly a roman fort there, and I suggest that he re-occupied that fort for a shorter or longer period because he was landless at least in the North. One might be tempted to think of the Camelot of the mediaeval historical fictions being derived from Camelon by the French romantic writers of the twelfth century. This may well be true but the Camelot of mediaeval romance tells us much about the twelfth century and next to nothing about the sixth. Whatever the truth, there is a rhyming between words such as Camelot and Lancelot, and these names seem to be mediaeval French interpolations into the Arthurian cycle, and they each belong in the strict sense to mediaeval fiction. Across the Carron from Camelon there was the beehive-shaped Roman shrine that I have already mentioned. It is now known as Arthur's O'n, and I remind readers this could at one time have provided a flat circular floor or tabulated rotunda for the meetings of Arthur's order of chivalry where they held their rites.

In this connection it is interesting to note that amongst the foreign mystery religions that thrived towards the tail end of the Roman Empire there was Mythraism, which was popular with the Roman military. In *Peredur* and the *Quest of the Grail* we find a mysterious procession which Jessie Weston, one of the most sensible commentators on the Grail quest, thought came from a rite of Mythraism. I must digress here because of a curious and interesting parallel; the layout of Christian churches seems to have taken its cue from that of Mythraic temples. One is tempted to wonder if Jesus had any contact with this cult during his 'lost years.' He said to the guardians of the temple in Jerusalem: 'you have the keys but you will not let anyone go in, and you will not go in yourselves.' This would imply that they had refused him the initiation into the Jewish mysteries and that he had had to look elsewhere, in other religions, for what he was seeking at that time. Jesus also said that 'if the salt hath lost its savour, wherewith shall it be salted,' implying a similar idea. The idea that the rites of the round table were of pagan origin does not mean that Arthur was not Christian. There are three basic ways in spirituality, of love, action and knowledge. Now Christianity provided, in particular in the monasteries, for those suited to follow a way of love; also a retreat for those seeking knowledge, although true intellectuals have been rare during the past two thousand years. This would leave those needing a way of action out in the cold, except that it seems likely that there was continuity of the existing spiritual practices of the warrior elite because their hidden practices were not incompatible with being a Christian.

Thus we have the possibility that Arthur was the spiritual head of an initiatic order of knights that held their rites on a flat circular floor. The demise of the Celtic church and its Romanisation, initiated by the Synod of Whitby in 664, followed by the Welsh acceptance of the Roman way of dating Easter in 768, possibly marked the beginning of the end of Celtic orders of spiritual chivalry. But it is note-worthy that in 1118 the Order of the Temple, better known as the Knights Templars, was founded with the blessing of St. Bernard. The function of the Templars was to guard the route to the Holy Land, which had a dual meaning, literally to guard the pilgrim route to Jerusalem, and more profoundly the secret way to the centre of one's own being, the God within mentioned by Jesus in the gospels. Jessie Weston spoke of a 'spiritual underground' possibly linking secret organisations in the Dark and Middle Ages, but it is impossible to say with certainty if the Templars had inherited anything from the ancient chivalry or not. Weston in particular mentions *Parzival,* a poem by Wolram von Eschenbach, where we find the grail in the care of a body of semi-militant knights who bear the significant name of Templeism, implying a link between Arthur's order of knights and the Templars. Although it is impossible to identify all the links in Jessie Weston's 'spiritual underground,' one can find interesting comparisons here and there, as we shall now see.

The Templar Church in Segovia in Spain has what is probably a unique construction. The interior of this church is circular and within it there is another circular wall so that between the two there is a circular walkway which functions as an aisle, there being an altar on one side. At ground-floor level the inner circle is filled in with masonry intersected by two tunnels at right angles to each other, thereby forming a cross within a circle. Above this block of masonry there is a flat circular stone floor, access being by a small stairway from the 'aisle' to a door through the inner wall at first floor height. Looking down from above, the plan of this building therefore follows the design of a Celtic wheel-cross with its centripetal symbolism. Furthermore, the floor above, within the central cylinder, would seem to suit the performance of a ritual by persons seated in a circle around a centre which would become for that purpose the world-centre or *axis mundi*. Although this alone proves nothing, the resemblance to the floor of Arthur's O'n cannot help but come to mind.

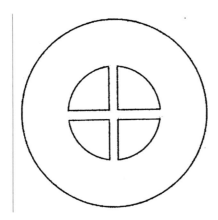

Layout of ground floor of the Templar church in Segovia; the altar is on the east; not to scale.

In an interesting article entitled *the Knights Templar and the Green man,* Tina Negus points out that foliate catheads, beast heads and human Green Men are a strong feature of many Templar churches in France and Britain. Negus says 'maybe the attributes of the cat family in particular – their power, mystery, independence, and their air of self-knowledge – had a special place in the Templar imagination.

*Neuvy-St-Sépulcre, Berry, France, 12ᵗʰ century capital of rotunda.
Cat or lioness head with mouth foliage.*

Speaking of the foliate heads in general she goes on to say that 'perhaps also they perceived in the image of the uttering head its deep meaning in terms of regeneration and rebirth, both of nature and of humanity, and its symbolic representation of the creation of the vegetative world upon which all life depends.' It is well worth noting that the greatest piece of Green Man literature in Britain is Arthurian; *Sir Gawain and the Green Knight,* and I shall say more about this topic later.

One of the striking features of the middle ages is the sudden appearance of magnificent Gothic cathedrals and churches with elaborate stone carvings and construction according to sacred geometrical designs. This sudden appearance lends support to Jessie Weston's idea of a spiritual underground.

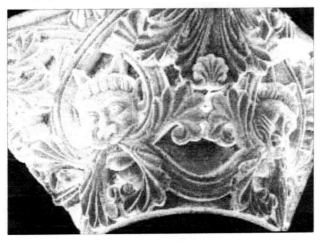

St Michael d'Entraygues, Angouleme, France. Capitol of octagonal 12th century church showing two of the three horned green men

Negus points out that the Templars gave much of the financial support for the Gothic building programme throughout Europe. She adds that 'some authors have attributed secret knowledge to them, for instance the architectural development of the Gothic Cathedrals, and the continuation of the mysteries of the Temple of Solomon in the rites of the Freemasons.' She adds that this may well be an over-statement, and I would add that the Freemasons began to lose their spiritual aspect quite some time after they had opened their doors to others who were not following the craft of a stone-mason. The symbolism of Masonry is said to have survived in its most intact form in Scotland. Tolstoy tried it in Russia in the nineteenth century and concluded that it had lost its spiritual content.

The Templars were very successful and were reputed to have great treasure. This led Philip le Bel of France, who was a big spender, to move against them in 1307. He had their leaders tortured so that they confessed to all sorts of heresies and perversions, but then the pope stepped in and said it was his trial. The pope had them re-arrested but not tortured and they withdrew all their confessions, and two witnesses, novices that had not entered the order, said that behind the walls of the Templar castles life was austere and pure. Philip however became so desperate for money that he intervened, had them tortured again, and burnt. The burning was slow and painful, not fast like the great conflagrations of the Hollywood films. It is not surprising that those who hung on to any real spirituality had to disguise or otherwise hide it.

Apart from the Templars, there were also the Cathars and Albigois in southern France that had survived independent of the Roman church until the thirteenth century. The pope uttered some words against them that triggered off the Albigensian Crusades in 1208. The nobles of northern France saw this as a land-grabbing opportunity sanctioned by the spiritual authority, and the 'crusades' ended some years later after the often genocidal destruction of the Cathar towns and cities. Some of those who escaped became the Troubadors and Trouvères that went about singing songs, often with a double meaning, hiding their Christian ideals of purity behind an apparent theme of love.

There may be something in the notion that the destruction of the Templars, the Albigensian Crusades, and the Inquisition inspired those with esoteric knowledge to hide their ideals in such works as *Sir Gawain and the Green Knight*, and the *Quest of the Grail*. Apart from Masonry, there were, in the Middle Ages, other craft initiatic societies that used the symbolism of their craft as a means of passing on spiritual knowledge. The last survival of such an organisation is said to the *Companionnage*, a guild of builders in timber in south-west France.

Now we can return to the Arthurian quest. Prior to the times of Geoffrey of Monmouth there were already within Arthuriana, poems and stories of the type of the spiritual quest. One is a poem known as *Preiddeu Annwn* which is commonly translated as the Spoils of Annwn. It is a poem of the *genre* of Jason and the Golden Fleece, but difficult to understand. It is in the Book of Taliesin, probably not earlier in composition than the late ninth century, but it could be based on pre-Christian tradition. It tells of a voyage of Arthur in his ship *Prydwen* to seize a magical cauldron in what is generally termed the 'otherworld.' There is good reason to consider this to be a poem of a spiritual quest to heaven, implying to the centre of one's own being, the God within, and the title should perhaps better be translated as the 'treasures of heaven, within,' taking *annwn* to mean 'heaven,' and I am indebted to Mr Wade Miller-Knight for this suggestion, and for pointing out that Taliesin normally dedicated each poem to one of his princely patrons, except for this one that was dedicated to God most high. Wade Miller-Knight has interpreted this poem according to the theory of Indian yoga, and he concludes that the first verse refers to people sitting in the correct posture for meditative practice, but his work is as yet unpublished.

The other is a story known as *Peredur*. In it the young Peredur seeks out Arthur and then goes on an adventure in which one of his uncles advises him not to ask any questions about anything he might see but not understand. Later, he sees a mysterious procession including in it a severed head on a platter, and a lance that drips blood. He asks no questions when in fact he should have done so despite his uncle's injunction; for he should have asked in order to discover that there was a mystery that he knew nothing about, a spiritual quest that he could undertake. The story ends with the anticlimax of a lame explanation that the mystery was about one of his relatives having been murdered by the nine sorceresses of Gloucester and that he should seek revenge. In fact, this story is almost certainly a re-write of a pre-Christian quest tale, perhaps of a magical cauldron kindled from the breath of nine virgins; Jessie Weston thought the strange procession in it may have originated from Mythraism. The Christian monks no doubt modified the ending of this story to permit its continued existence; and they may also have Arthurianized the whole tale for the same reason, Arthur being a recognized Christian hero and Peredur, later Percival, one of his knights.

So there was in the pre-Galfredian Arthurian literature already the idea of the spiritual quest. Coe and Young, along with other writers all consider the above-mentioned poem, and the story of Peredur as probable precursors of the *Quest of the Grail,* which includes what in the classical world were known as the lesser mysteries (of the twice-born) and the greater mysteries (leading across the seven heavens to union with God). Also there was the story of *Sir Gawain and the Green knight* with its emphasis on purity, self control and chastity; a story that has been described as the very epitome of religion.

The Green Knight or Green Man is known throughout the world as the eternal prophet; in early Christianity he seems to have become confounded with St. George which is why he is no longer known by his original name in the West except on inn signs. The story of *Sir Gawain and the Green Knight* is set in Arthur's court, perhaps in the early days, for his knights are described as 'berdless childer.' The geography of it seems to belong to north-east Wales and the adjacent parts of England. The story begins with a knight appearing at Arthur's court and challenging any-one to a contest of mutual head-chopping. Gawain answers the challenge and chops off his head, which the decapitated body picks up and the head tells him to meet him for his part of the bargain in a year and a day at the Green Chapel. The story continues with Gawain's ad-ventures as he travels in search of the Green Chapel. To-wards the end of the year he comes upon a castle where he receives hospitality from the lord who makes a bargain with him that he will go hunting for each of three days and present Gawain with whatever he catches whereas Gawain will stay and rest with the lady of the castle and give the lord whatever he has received during the day. During two days Gawain resists the temptation of the beautiful lady, but on the third they kiss and she gives him a silk scarf. When the lord of the castle returns on the third evening Gawain is obliged to kiss him as his part of the bargain, but he does not tell him about the gift of green silk. The next day is the one of the final showdown. Gawain goes to the Green Chapel and meets the lord of the castle now as the Green Knight. It is Gawain's turn to place his head on the block. Three times the Green Knight brings down his enormous axe, missing his neck twice, but just nicking it enough to bleed on the third time. He tells Gawain that the small wound on his neck is because he kept the gift of the green silk from his wife a secret from him. Then he tells Gawain to arise absolved and clean of sin as he was on the day he was born. Needless to say this implies that Gawain thereby becomes one of the twice-born, a True Man. Thus this is a story of honesty, purity, self-control and chastity, for the sake of spiritual liberation. Although a work of mediaeval fiction, albeit truth-bearing in its symbolism, this tale may be based on earlier tradition. The geography in it fits into the scenery of North-West Wales. The Castle could be *Castell Dinas Brân* near Llangollen, and the Green Chapel would appear to be Eglwysig Mountain (Ecclesiastical Mountain) a green hill on the eastern side of the Vale of Llangollen. The 'desert' where Gawain wanders for some time in his quest is thought to be the Wirral where there were no settlements; just a few hermit-saints and outlaws. The dramatic scenery of World's End at the northern end of the Vale of Llangollen could be the final meeting place where Gawain places his head on the block.

The *Quest of the Holy Grail*, in a sense the *magnum opus* of Arthurian literature, is literally about Arthur's knights going out in search of the grail as a physical object having wonderful properties of a spiritual nature. The knights are sent out on this quest by Arthur telling them that the time is right for them to do so. He does not go himself. Stories of this type are seldom intended to be understood literally, fantastic and enjoyable as they may be to read. It is just possible that the vessel used to hold the blood of Jesus at the crucifixion did exist as a physical object with wonderful properties; there used to be a wooden bowl called the holy grail in West Wales that was said to have curative properties when anyone drank water from it, but which lost its power after someone fitted a silver rim to it. But the real import of the Quest is to be understood as a journey to the centre of ones being, the God within of the Gospels. This takes us back to the symbolism of the heart mentioned earlier in this chapter. Reaching the outside of the heart corresponds with achieving the lesser mysteries, the twice-born state of true man. Going on to the centre of the heart implies the greater mysteries corresponding with the seven heavens, and on to union with God Thus I put it that the quest of the grail, in reality, is the quest of one's heart, the God within. In the story of the quest, which I do not intend to go over in detail here, many of Arthur's knights fail. Lancelot sees the outside of the grail, and then loses consciousness; when he recovers he is told that seeing the outside of the grail is as much of the quest as he shall achieve in his lifetime. I put it to the reader that this means that he had reached the knowledge of the outside of the heart, the state of True Man, twice-born, but he could go no further. Perceval, on the other hand takes the grail to the East where he becomes its guardian until one day he looks inside it and begins to see spiritual things; he is so filled with ecstatic wonder that he asks God to deliver him from this life there and then, and in the story, the grail was taken up into heaven and no one since then has ventured to claim they have seen it. I apologise to readers that like to have the idea that one simply has to take possession of an exterior object to gain wonderful knowledge and experience, but the spiritual life

143

does not go like that. Those who wish can take the story literally, but in terms of heart symbolism, Percival's looking inside the grail can be taken as referring to experiencing the inside of the heart, the 'journey' across the seven heavens that culminates in union with God.

It is unlikely that Jason's Golden Fleece, the various magical cauldrons that are to be found in Celtic quest tales, and the Grail, ever existed as physical objects. There are two possible reasons for hiding esoteric knowledge in such a story, firstly because there is a danger of ancient knowledge becoming lost and forgotten during the declining cycle of time when the majority have lost their spiritual orientation through worldliness; and secondly because ordinary people cannot understand profound truths and will oppose them, just as established religious or political power blocks may wish to eradicate such knowledge. In addition, to set down knowledge of the esoteric quest in a dry text or a book like this one, would not permit it to last, whereas if the same ideas can be hidden in a game or a good story that will please generations of young children aged six to sixty or more, then they can go on indefinitely.

10. A LIFE OF ARTHUR

In writing this largely imaginary Life of Arthur I am not saying that this is history as it actually happened; it is just an attempt to explain the possible reality or meaning behind some aspects of the legends, such as the sword in the stone, Arthur's "coronation," his campaign against the "Saxons," and his subsequent life in what is now North Wales, ending in the famous Battle of Camlan. For the account up to the period of his coronation I have followed the Welsh version of the Birth of Arthur in Y Cymroddor, Vol. XXIV which can be found reprinted in *Pendragon* by Blake and Lloyd; it is late, from the fifteenth century, but it may contain some Welsh traditions independent of the Brut. It is not certain that Cynyr was the person that fostered Arthur, but I have kept this in the absence of any better suggestion. For Arthur's battles I have followed the Brut, using the revised interpretations of place-names based on the Welsh text up to the Battle of Breidden and on to Alclyde. I think a Welsh region scenario for a battle-campaign up to the one of Badon clears up more problems than it creates in terms of the geography in the old histories, though many may disagree. I think also that it is reasonable to retain a Scottish episode at the end of Arthur's campaign at the present state of knowledge. For events leading to the Battle of Camlan I have used the Welsh Triads. For those following the Battle of Camlan I have followed Michael Lapidge's translation of the *Vera Historia De Morte Arthuri*. The oldest manuscript of this is of the fourteenth century, but it may have first been written around the year 1200 and it contains material that is not in Geoffrey or the Brut. As I said at the beginning, the last word on this subject may never be written, and the aim of this chapter is simply to try to uncover a little of the fire behind the smoke.

Uthyr Pendragon, Arthur's legendary father, was the equivalent of the *Dux Bellorum* or battle-leader of the Romans. He seems to have been involved in the in-fighting that the

Britons had reverted to after the collapse of Roman power, and he might have been chosen as battle-leader of the Britons following on after Ambrosius. He probably wore the diadem that was worn by just a few of the principal warriors. This diadem was not a magnificent royal crown, but a slender golden hoop that could be worn around the head. Young warriors would go into battle each with a golden torque around their neck for bravado, to tempt the enemy to have a go at them. A diadem would serve the same function. Uthyr is said to have had a golden dragon carried on a standard before him when he went into battle, hence his name of Pendragon or Dragonhead. Although Dragonhead was Arthur's natural father, this child was going to be born so soon after his marriage that the people would not regard him as his legitimate successor.

From the time of his birth, Arthur was therefore fostered by another lord, Cynyr Farfog, and brought up along with his own son Cei that he regarded as his brother. Arthur was given not book learning, but an education based on oral tradition and the good use of language, along with practice in horsemanship and the martial arts of that time. He also learnt about military tactics, including those that had been used by the Roman army. At fourteen or fifteen he would have been considered ready to bear arms, and he would have entered into the *teulu*, literally family, but meaning war-band of his lord. He may have received an initiation into the secret spiritual tradition of the warrior class, perhaps derived from the esoteric side of Mythraism which had been favoured by the Roman military.

Dragonhead had died, but not before asking a holy abbot to look out for his son that had been adopted. This left

146

the Britons without a war-leader. The Abbot, who some say was Dubricius, knew that it would be near impossible to persuade the British 'kings' to agree among themselves as to whom should be chosen; so he set to making preparations for a plan that had formed in his mind, for he thought it would be best if an unknown young warrior who was not one of them were to be accepted. He sent some of his monks on a long journey to bring a large slab of marble looking quite different from the local stone where the lords were to meet.

The Abbot set his plan into motion by inviting the British nobility to a meeting to choose a new military commander, and he made sure that Cynyr would bring Cai and Arthur. The meeting started off in uproar, so the Abbot addressed them all, saying "let us first spend some time in church in prayer so that we can discuss this in a calm atmosphere." This they did; and no one noticed a small newly-dug grave with no pile of earth beside it. On resuming the discussion, the same squabbling continued. Then the Abbot said "let us go back into the Church and pray to the Almighty to send us a sign so that we may know whom we should choose." After they had spent quite some time in the church, and the people began to leave, those still inside heard the words "A miracle! A miracle!" and sure enough outside there was a large and very heavy slab of a polished stone such as few had seen before. There was a sword sticking out of the stone, and an inscription on the latter in the Briton tongue and Latin to the effect that he who should withdraw the sword would be the rightful war-leader of the Britons.

Once again, the Abbot said they should go back into the church to thank the Lord for having vouchsafed a sign for

147

them. When they came out, several of the noble warriors tried to pull out the sword, but in vain, and, as night was falling, the Abbot said they should all go to sleep, and try again tomorrow after prayers. He appointed a few of his monks and close friends to keep guard over the wonderful stone for the night. Towards daybreak, whilst everyone else was still asleep, more monks came and joined the night-watchmen and between them they lifted the stone slab whilst one of them went down into the trench below. The slab was lowered back in place but with a few inconspicuous channels to allow air to circulate and so that the monk below could hear what was being said outside.

In the morning everyone indulged in sword-play and such like activities before going into the church. Afterwards they tried without success, one after the other, to pull out the stone. So the Abbot invited them back for more prayer. Cynyr had broken his sword at the hilt in a mock sword fight with someone who seemed bent on breaking it, and he sent Arthur to his lodgings to fetch his spare sword. He could not find it, but on the way back he saw the sword in the stone, pulled it out and took it to Cynyr who at first thought to pretend it was he who had done it, but he had second thoughts as he would look a fool if he could not do it again. He told the others, and everyone went outside to confirm that the sword was no longer there. In a voice loud and clear the Abbot asked Arthur to put the sword back, which he did; then he asked one or two warriors to try to pull it out, but they could not, then Arthur was asked to try and he succeeded without effort. This was repeated again on two other agreed dates with the same result, and on the last occasion the Abbot said they should go back into the church to give thanks to God for having chosen them a war-lord. Once they were in the church, a couple of monks stood guard outside the door to give the alarm should anyone try to come out, and a party of monks appeared, released the monk that had operated the clamp, and carried off the stone and made it disappear into a large grave at the back of the churchyard. Then they brought back the tubs of earth that had been concealed beneath some hay, filled in the trench and carefully replaced the turves in true boy-scout fashion and watered them so that there was no sign that a hole had ever been dug there. When all this was completed, the monks disappeared except for the two guarding the church door. They gave a sign to someone inside and shortly after the people came out to find that the stone had disappeared just as miraculously as it had come.

The Abbot obtained the general consent of the lords to appoint Arthur as battle-chief of all the Britons. Most of the lords were content that it was not one of their enemies amongst the British aristocracy that had been appointed, and those who had doubts about Arthur as a potential war leader were reassured on hearing a rumour that he was the natural son of old Dragonhead. Once again, the Abbot invited them all to meet in church where Arthur was 'crowned' not with a royal crown, but the diadem of a chief warrior, a slender golden hoop that was worn around the head as a symbol of office. Such diadems are mentioned in one of the Welsh Triads, and one of those entitled to wear one was his foster-brother Cei.

It is possible, even likely, that Arthur had been brought up under a different name, and that he only acquired the name we know him by at this time. It was given him by the Abbot as one that would suit both Romanised Britons and the wilder ones from the mountains that did not

149

speak Latin.   At this time the Abbot informed him that he had been fostered and who his natural father was. This enabled Arthur perhaps to claim some inheritance which had been watched over by the Abbot on his behalf.

Young Arthur was skilled in oratory, conversation and the military arts. He was generous and likeable, and soon he attracted to himself a *teulu* meaning a 'family' or band of young warriors, all skilled at fighting on horseback. Clearly Arthur had something intangible about him, perhaps a hidden spiritual quality that attracted so many to him.   But he was generous and whatever patrimony he may have had did not support his expenditure.

Soon after his coronation he led his war-band together with soldiers provided by the other kings or chiefs and conducted a successful campaign against the Saxons who had occupied the lands from coast to coast along the eastern fringe of the lands of the South Britons, and were penetrating into Wales. In the middle of this campaign he received news of more Saxons landing in the north, and he sent a request to his nephew Howel for military aid to deal with this escalating situation. Together they went on and defeated the Saxons and drove them into the great forest where they hemmed them in by constructing an enclosure round them. They surrendered and agreed to give hostages and all their loot and go back to their original homes. Howel set out by sea for Alcluyd which was threatened by Picts and Scots, and Arthur was about to follow him by road; but once out at sea the Saxons changed their minds, and came back.

Arthur learnt that they were established on a fortified hill called Breidden, some miles north across the ford on the

Severn at modern Buttington near Welshpool. He and his friend Cador took each their cavalry with them; a bunch of youths that had no family ties and would charge wildly into the midst of the enemy with no thought of danger. Arthur told half of his troops to keep out of sight under the trees, and he and half of his youths took up position behind their shield wall and taunted the Saxons, daring them to come down and do battle. Seeing only a small body of very young and inexperienced warriors, and realising that Arthur was not accompanied by the more mature forces of the other British kings, the Saxons said "We've got more weight and strength than they have; lets go down and show these kids what's what;" and they came down the hill behind their shield wall with the confidence that they would be easy meat. But no sooner were the two sides lined up facing each other than Arthur and his warriors melted away back to their horses, and before they knew what was happening the Saxons were being run down by a cavalry charge of those of Arthur's band that had remained mounted and out of sight. Arthur and his front line soon joined them on horseback but the Saxons that survived this onslaught managed to climb back to the security of the hilltop. The next day Arthur and his men stormed the hill and won a great victory that gave him possession of the lands along the eastern fringe of the Wales of that time. Arthur left his friend Cador to pursue and run down the remaining Saxons. And that was the famous Battle of Breidden, Beidon or Badon.

[Arthur's success against the Saxons was probably attributable to his use of cavalry whenever possible. The Saxons seem to have fought on foot and with spears. Although they could throw their spears with lethal effect, they were probably reluctant to do so against cavalry for

151

they would not have much chance of retrieving them; and that would leave them defenceless and easy to run down. — Foot soldiers never stopped a cavalry charge until the Battle of Falkirk when Wallace used the stratagem of long pointed poles with their rear ends fixed in the ground, and which could be raised suddenly to horse-breast height.]

Then Arthur and his band took the road north to where Howel was besieged by Picts and Scots at Dumbarton; he and his cavalry charged into the camp of the besiegers, driving the Picts back to their ships, and the Scots to Loch Lomond where they surrendered. Next he secured the castle at Edinburgh, and his contention there seems to have ended in an amicable settlement. Then he won a battle outside Stirling, so that the three great fortresses of what is now Southern Scotland were safely in the hands of the Britons. But whilst he was in the North he made his camp in the ruins of the Roman fort at Camelon where his men could relax for a time. Whilst there, Arthur and some of his close associates used the old Roman monument across the river for meditation purposes and the practice of any secret ritual that had come down to them from the mysteries of Mithraism. The season for wars in the old days was the autumn, after the crops had been harvested and when the ground was firm and dry so that horses and men would not get bogged down in the mud. Even if they had achieved their objective quickly it would have been too late to travel back and they would have been obliged to over-winter at Camelon, with a view to travelling the following spring or summer, and during that period Arthur would have held his "court" there.

It has been said that from then onwards Arthur spent most of his time in North Wales. He seems to have occupied the hillfort above Penrhyn Bay, near Rhyl in North Wales, and there he held his court for some time. That hillfort is called Dinarth or the Fort of the Bear, perhaps named after Arthur himself. During this period in Wales he lived variously with the three wives and three mistresses accredited him by the Welsh Triads. This was a time for entertaining guests, hunting and feasting and playing games, and sending his followers off in search of adventures. Possibly during this period, if not before, he became seriously involved in the spiritual quest, as we are told in the poem *Preiddeu Annwn* or the Treasures of Heaven. This poem speaks of Arthur going in his ship on a quest to the 'otherworld,' a heaven where there is a cauldron kindled from the breath of nine virgins. And that of many that went only seven returned. The ship implies crossing the 'lower waters' of Genesis, the bodily and psychic realms, to the 'upper waters' of the spiritual realm, obtaining the state of one 'twice-born' and beyond.

But it seems that he lost Dinarth and its lands, and Gildas says that in his time it was occupied by one Cuneglassus. This loss is hinted at in an old poem by J. Finglwyd:

"Arthur ydwyd wrth rodiau
    Aeth ei waid unwaith o'i law."

"Thy gait is like that of Arthur,
    Who once lost his kingdom."

So he went to offer his services perhaps to Caswallon Lawhir, but probably his successor Maelgwn who is said to have fought many battles and killed many kings in achieving his ambition of becoming ruler of Gwynedd. Arthur was welcomed and given a suitable *Din* or fort at

Gelliwig on the Lleyn as a residence for himself and his retinue because of his reputation. From then onwards any battles he was involved in were against other groups of South Britons.

After many years, a quarrel arose between Gwenhwyfar, Arthur's wife, and her sister Gwenhwyfach who seems to have been Medrawd's wife. At night in bed they each began to turn their husband against his former friend. The dispute had begun, and the flames were fanned by other evil tongues that whispered gossip and lies into the ears of Arthur and Medrawd. Eventually a row broke out, inflamed by the passions that are aroused when friendship and love turn to hatred, and the two sides agreed to meet for a final showdown on the plain of the River Dovey by the slope called Camlan. The first day the battle followed the rules of war but even so some of the young men fell on each side. The sight of the bodies of these much-loved friends and relatives further inflamed the passions of each side so that on the second day the battle was bloody and vengeful, and by the third day it had turned into a fight to the finish, in which both Arthur and Medrawd fell, and there were few survivors; some say four, others seven.

The *Vera Historia* says that at the end of the battle a young man rode up to Arthur and threw a spear, inflicting an even more deadly wound on him. Some say that he died and was buried in a cave; but nobody says where. Others say that he asked to be taken to Gwynnedd to the land of Avallach to have his wound healed by his half-sister who was skilled in the seven arts. When she saw his wound she said that it would take weeks to heal and that he would be dead long before that. Therefore, she proposed to give him a medicine that would make him unconscious indefinitely, so that he could stay alive until the healing process was complete. Some say that he is still sleeping in his cave to come back at a critical time when he will be most needed, but others believe this was wishful thinking on the part of the Welsh; but the real import of this myth is probably that the spiritual and other qualities of the Age of Arthur will be restored one day. [In the book of the *Physicians of Myddfai*, curiously enough, there is a claim that those physicians had means of rendering a patient unconscious for several days until he or she had recovered from an operation].

Shakespeare seems to have thought that Arthur was dead, for when Falstaff died he said that he was in "Arthur's bosom." Cervantes who was Shakespeare's contemporary said that Arthur was going about the land of Britain in the form of a raven. Perhaps the mortally wounded Arthur was cared for in *Castell Dinas Brân* in the Vale of Llangollen. There is a tradition there that the keeper of the castle used to be warned by a talking raven of any hostile forces in the neighbourhood. It is further said that visitors to that castle in the middle ages had to go up the hill with a basket or bucket over their heads to avoid bombardment by hordes of black birds. The ravens in the Tower of London are said to be descended from those of *Castell Dinas Brân*.

REFERENCES

Alcock, Leslie, *Arthur's Britain,* London, 1971.

Annals of Clonmacnoise, the. Ed. E. D. Murphy, translated in 1617; facsimile of 1896 ed. Llanerch, Felinfach,

Baring-Gould and Fisher *Lives of the British Saints* reprint Llanerch Felinfach 1999.

Bartrum, P. C., *A Welsh Classical Dictionary,* Aberystwyth, 1995.

Blake, Steve, and Lloyd, Scot. *Pendragon; The Definitive Account of the Origins of Arthur.* London, 2000

Boece, Hector, *The Chronicle of Scotland,* Edinburgh, 1540; reprint 1977.

Bond, J. F., *A Handy Book of Rules and Tables for Verifying Dates.* 1869, Llanerch Reprint., 1995

Brown, I. G., and Vasey, P. G., *Arthur's O'n again: newly-discovered drawings by John Adair, and their context.* Proc. Soc. Antiquaries of Scotland, vol. 119, 1989.

Bryce, Derek, *The Mystical Way and the Arthurian Quest,* Samuel Weiser, York Beach, 1996. (Reprinted as *the Way and the Quest,* Llanerch, Cribyn, 2005)

Chadwick, Nora, *The British Heroic Age,* Cardiff, 1976.

Coe, John, B. and Young, Simon, *the Celtic Sources for the Arthurian Legend,* Llanerch, Felinfach, 1995.

Collingwood, R. G., *Roman Britain and the English Settlements,* O.U.P., Oxford, 1937.

Crawford, *Arthur and his Battles,* Antiquity IX, 1935.

Davies, John. *The Celtic Element of the English People,* collected papers from *Archaeologia Cambrensis,* Llanerch 2004.

Dumville, David N., *Celtic-Latin texts in Northern England, c. 1150—c. 1250.* Celtica, Vol. 12, 1977.

Geoffrey of Monmouth. *The History of the Kings of Britain,* trans. Lewis Thorpe, Penguin, London, 1966.

Gibbs, Ray, *The Legendary Twelve Hides of Glastonbury,* Llanerch, Felinfach, 1986.

Gildas, *The Ruin of Britain,* Michael Winterbottom, Phillimore, London, 1978.

Gildas, *two Lives of,* in Williams, Hugh, 1899; reprint: Llanerch, 1990.

Giles, J. A. *Six Old English Chronicles,* London, 1848.

Gita – see: *The Geeta,* English trans. Shri Purohit Swami, Faber, London, 1945.

— see also *The Bhagavad Gita,* trans. Juan Mascaro, Penguin, London, 1962

Glennie, John S. Stuart, *Arthurian Localities, their historical origin, chief country, and Fingalian relations; with a map of Arthurian Scotland,* 1869, Llanerch, Felinfach, facsimile 1994.

Gordon, J. *Itinerarum Septentrionale,* 1726.

Griffen, Toby, D. *Names from the Dawn of British Legend,* Llanerch, Felinfach, 1994.

Hardwick, Charles, *Ancient Battle Fields in Lancashire.* Abel Heywood, Manchester, 1882.

Henry of Huntingdon, *The Chronicle of,* trans. Thomas Forester, Llanerch reprint, Felinfach, 1991.

Jackson, A.O.H. *The Gododdin: The Oldest Scottish Poem*. Edinburgh University Press, 1969.

Jackson, A.O.H. *Arthur's Battle of Bregouin*, Antiquity, 23, 1949.

Johnson, Paul, *A History of Christianity*, Penguin, London, 1990.

Lapidge, Michael, *Vera Historia De Morte Arthuri*, in Carley, J.P., *Glastonbury Abbey and the Arthurian Tradition*, 2001.

Loth, Ferdinand, *Nennius et L'Historia Brittonum*, Paris, 1934.

Mabinogion, the Four Branches, trans, Charlotte Guest, Llanerch, Felinfach, 1994.

Meddygon Myddfai. The Physicians of Myddfai, John Pughe. Facsimile reprint by Llanerch Press, 1995.

Morris, John (ed.), Nennius, *British History and the Welsh Annals*, London, Phillimore, 1980.

Myvirian Archaiology (Jones, Pugh and Williams), London 1801.

Padel, O. J., *The Nature of Arthur* Cambrian Medieval Studies 27 (Summer 1994).

Palmer, Martin with Brenilly, Elizabeth, *the Book of Chuang Tzu* Penguin, London.

Pennar, Meirion, *Taliesin Poems*, Llanerch, 1988.

Pennar, Meirion, *The Black Book of Carmarthen*, Llanerch, Felinfach, 1989.

Pennar, Meirion, *Peredur*, translated from the *White Book Mabinogion*, Llanerch, Felinfach, 1986.

Philokalia, the, ed. G.E.H. Palmer et al, Faber, London, 1981.